The Ultimate Vatican City Guide

Keenan .W Dickerson

All rights reserved. Copyright © 2023 Keenan .W Dickerson

COPYRIGHT © 2023 Keenan .W Dickerson

All rights reserved.

No part of this book must be reproduced, stored in a retrieval system, or shared by any means, electronic, mechanical, photocopying, recording, or otherwise, without written permission from the publisher.

Every precaution has been taken in the preparation of this book; still the publisher and author assume no responsibility for errors or omissions. Nor do they assume any liability for damages resulting from the use of the information contained herein.

Legal Notice:

This book is copyright protected and is only meant for your individual use. You are not allowed to amend, distribute, sell, use, quote or paraphrase any of its part without the written consent of the author or publisher.

Introduction

Welcome to this book, a portal to one of the world's most revered and culturally significant destinations. This guidebook is your personal key to unlocking the hidden gems, awe-inspiring artistry, and profound spirituality that reside within the Vatican's historic walls.

Our journey begins by exploring the captivating surroundings of the Vatican, setting the stage for your visit to this sacred enclave. You'll encounter St. Peter's Basilica, a breathtaking architectural marvel that has transcended time as a symbol of faith and devotion.

As you step through the Vatican's entrance, you'll be transported into a world where art, history, and spirituality converge. Each corridor and hall you traverse is steeped in centuries of heritage and adorned with artistic treasures that will leave you spellbound.

Within the Vatican's tranquil Cortile della Pigna, or Pinecone Courtyard, you can pause to appreciate the serene beauty that contrasts with the bustling energy of the Vatican's daily life.

The Vatican's commitment to preserving and displaying artistic excellence is exemplified in the Galleria della Candelabra. Here, you'll be immersed in the grandeur of candelabra and surrounded by masterpieces of creative genius.

Step into the Gallery of the Tapestries, where magnificent tapestries unfold stories of antiquity before your eyes, inviting you to become part of their narratives.

In the Gallery of the Maps, the intricate details of historical maps will transport you through time and geography, showcasing the Vatican's dedication to knowledge and exploration.

Raphael's Rooms offer a glimpse into the brilliance of this celebrated Renaissance artist, whose masterpieces evoke a sense of wonder and transport you to a bygone era.

As you make your way towards the Sistine Chapel, the anticipation of experiencing one of the world's most renowned artistic achievements heightens the journey itself.

The Sistine Chapel ceiling, adorned with Michelangelo's breathtaking frescoes, is a sight that defies description. Prepare to be overwhelmed by the awe-inspiring beauty and historical significance of this masterpiece.

Finally, Michelangelo's "The Last Judgment" on the Sistine Chapel's altar wall adds another layer of grandeur and spirituality to your visit, leaving an indelible mark on your memory.

In this book, we invite you to embark on a journey of discovery and reverence. Whether you are a seasoned traveler or a first-time visitor, this guidebook will enhance your experience, offering insights into the Vatican's history, art, and spiritual significance. Join us as we explore the Vatican's timeless wonders, one magnificent destination at a time.

Contents

1. OVERVIEW 1
2. AROUND THE VATICAN 3
3. ST. PETER'S BASILICA 17
4. VATICAN MUSEUMS 1: ENTRANCE 43
5. THE VATICAN MUSEUMS 2: CORTILE DELLA PIGNA 48
6. THE VATICAN MUSEUMS 3: GALLERIA DELLA CANDELABRA 68
7. THE VATICAN MUSEUMS 4: GALLERY OF THE TAPESTRIES 71
8. THE VATICAN MUSEUMS 5: GALLERY OF THE MAPS 75
9. THE VATICAN MUSEUM 6: RAPHAEL'S ROOMS 81
10. THE VATICAN MUSEUM 7: TOWARDS THE SISTINE CHAPEL ...96
11. THE VATICAN MUSEUMS 8: THE SISTINE CHAPEL CEILING 98
12. THE VATICAN MUSEUMS 9: THE LAST JUDGMENT 124

1. OVERVIEW

This book will help you if you plan on visiting the Vatican or want to know more about it. The Vatican is an enormous place, full of artwork and history. It can even be a bit overwhelming when you visit it. Saint Peter's Basilica is filled with baroque sculptures, the Vatican Museums have art from all time periods and the Sistine Chapel and the Raphael Rooms have the most beautiful Fresco's in the world.

    Visiting such a place can be an amazing, once in a lifetime experience. You can make the most out of your visit by preparing it a bit. Believe me, the Vatican will make so much more sense to you if you know some of the best stories about the art and the people that created it. If you don't know what to look at, it can be really too much.

    In my Vatican guide book, I will show you exactly what to pay attention to. You will know exactly which artworks are considered the most important and you will know the often amazing stories behind their creation. I also included a lot of must-know tips for visitors, which will make your stay a pleasant one. Maybe you have heard of the long lines and the hours people have to wait before entering Saint Peter's or the Vatican Museums and Sistine Chapel? I will give you some tips on how to avoid these lines, and much more.

    I wrote this book as a complete guide to the Vatican. It describes the most important artworks you can find inside the Vatican. I am a tour guide in the Vatican Museums and the city of Rome itself. Besides this I also work all over Italy as a tour guide. I found that most guidebooks people have only provide very general information. Just a few hotel and restaurant recommendations and descriptions of the monuments with lots of pictures. This guidebook is completely different. It is for those people that want to have a much more profound knowledge about the Vatican and its monuments. In it, you will find detailed descriptions and maps of the Vatican museums, Saint Peter's Basilica and Vatican City. I use this book as a reference for my work as a tour guide. I hope it will give you a deep understanding of all the beautiful statues, fresco's, tapestries and paintings in this amazing place.

At the start of each chapter you will find maps. The numbers on the maps correspond with the section numbers in the book. For example, Michelangelo's Pietà is described in section 3.3, which means it can be located on the map at the beginning of chapter 3 at number 3.

2. AROUND THE VATICAN

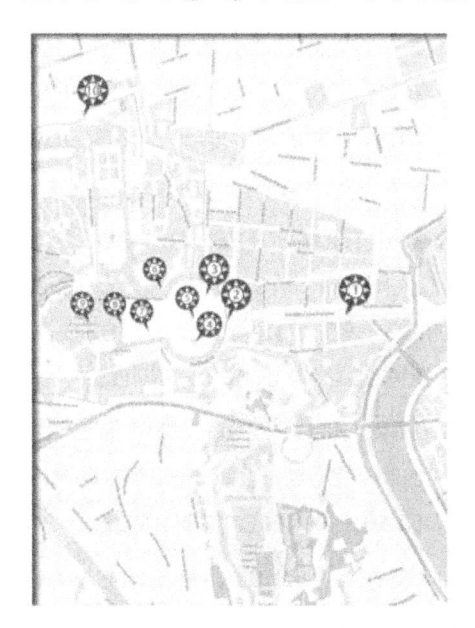

First off, let's start with some tips for visiting the Vatican. Make sure to book your tickets to the Vatican museums in advance on the official website of the Vatican. The website is www.vatican.va. The lines to the museums can be much too long in the high season which runs from April until November. It's not fun spending hours in line and with an online ticket you can just enter through the special gate for advance bookers. You have to pay a bit more for the tickets, but it is really worth it.

If you didn't book your ticket in advance, I would try to get in at lunch time. Most guidebooks advise you to go early in the morning and that is what most people do, so the lines are really long. At lunch you might have a better chance to get in quicker. Another option is to reserve your visit for later in the afternoon. The lines to get in are most definitely much shorter, but of course you will have less time to see everything. This is a good option if you just want to see the highlights like the Sistine Chapel.

You can have a cheap lunch inside the Vatican Museums. The price is much lower than the restaurants in the area around the Vatican. You can get a full lunch, but they also sell sandwiches and slices of Pizza.

You can take pictures anywhere inside the museums, except the Sistine Chapel. In some areas no flash is allowed. Make sure to turn off your flash, as the guards will get angry at you if you take a picture with flash in these areas (like the gallery of the tapestries).

Beware of pickpockets inside the Museums and especially inside the Sistine Chapel. On normal days it is really busy and everybody is looking up at the ceiling, so some pickpockets take advantage.

Make sure to take this guidebook with you. Just make sure you come prepared, so you know at least a bit what you are looking at.

Many people take the Metro to go to the Vatican. It is the easiest way, unless your hotel is close or you are willing to pay for a taxi. Rome's metro system is very straightforward. There are only a few lines, of which the A line and the B line are most useful. You will need to get on the A line and get off at metro stop Ottaviano. From here it is a short walk to the Vatican.

When you get close to the Vatican or when you get out the Metro, many people will approach you, to try to sell tours of the Vatican. Many customers are very unsatisfied with these tours. The promotors will tell you anything to get you to sign up, because they work on a commission. They will often get about 10 euros for each customer they bring in. So when they say a tour leaves right away, don't believe them. If you want a guided tour to the Vatican, I would get one beforehand on the internet with a company that has a great reputation on TripAdvisor.

After you finished touring the Vatican, have an ice-cream at Gelateria Oldbridge, Viale Bastioni di Michelangelo 5. It's next to the walls of the Vatican. They make their own ice cream in the back. Often you see lines of Italians and tourists outside, waiting to be served. It's definitely worth the short wait.

I always like to get a cheap slice of good pizza at Pizza Rustica ai Gracchi, at 6 Via dei Gracchi. This is a side street of Via Ottaviano, the shopping street that goes from the metro stop to the Vatican. This is not an overpriced touristy pizza place like everywhere else around the Vatican. Just nice slices of pizza. You can't sit here, but you are close to Piazza del Risorgimento, where you can sit on one of the benches or walls. The Pizza is *al taglio* here, which is a typical Roman way of selling slices of pizza. You just indicate how much you want and the lady will cut it. The price is determined according to the weight of the slice.

If you like your coffee not overpriced, you can always get your coffee *da portare via*. You might already know that the prices for sitting down and standing at the bar are different in Italy. It's often very expensive to sit down to drink coffee at touristy places like around the Vatican, but standing at the bar is cheap. I ask to take away my coffee. They'll charge standing prices and I'll just sit at Piazza Risorgimento.

If you had enough of all the beautiful art, there is a shopping street going from Piazza di Risorgimento back to the city center. It's called Via Cola di Rienzo and you will not see too many tourists on it.

2.1 Via della Conciliazione

Image 1

The wide road leading to the Vatican is called the Via della Concilazione. It means Reconciliation Street. It was built between 1936 and 1950. Before, there was a block of houses here and lots of small streets. The name refers to the reconciliation of the church and the Italian state, which resulted in the Lateran treaty of 1929. In this treaty between Mussolini and the Pope, the boundaries of Vatican City were drawn. To build this street, many houses and churches were torn down. On both sides of the street you can see many obelisks. The Romans call these jokingly suppositories.

2.2 Introduction to the Vatican

Image 2 "Photo by DAVID ILIFF. License: CC-BY-SA 3.0"

When you are standing on Saint Peter's square, you are inside the Vatican. So first of, let's talk a bit about how this very small country came to be. When the Western Roman Empire fell in 476 AD Italy entered difficult times. Many different barbarians invaded the peninsula, like the Goths, the Vandals and the Huns. There was no more emperor in Rome and different barbarian kings ruled parts of Italy. So the Bishop of Rome, the Pope, became the de facto ruler of the city and in the next few centuries the power of the papacy grew immensely. Another factor that contributed to the Pope's power was the habit of many rich people to leave their land to the papacy after they died, to secure a place in heaven. Slowly the Pope became the ruler of most of the land around Rome. This was the beginning of the Papal States. The Papal States were comprised of what are now the Umbria and Lazio regions. These lands remained in the possession of the pope until 1870 when the country Italy was created. The Papal States were conquered and added to the new country. After this, Rome was declared the capital of the new Italian kingdom. The Pope at the time, Pius IX, was so upset that he locked himself up inside the Vatican City and never left again.

The legal status of the Vatican was made clear many years later in 1929 in the Lateran Treaty between the Kingdom of Italy and the Holy See. Pope Pius XI and Mussolini drew the borders of the Vatican. It became a separate country inside Italy, with its own laws and regulations. The Pope wanted to keep the Vatican state as small as possible, because he felt that earlier Popes had been distracted from their religious functions, because they were also temporal rulers. So the Vatican state is now comprised of everything inside the Leonine walls, but also of a few very important churches in the city like Saint John of Lateran and Santa Maria Maggiore. Also the Papal Palace in Castelgandolfo is Vatican territory.

So now the Vatican is a very small country. It has its own postal service. If you want to send postcards from Italy it is a lot smarter to use the Vatican post, because it is a lot more efficient. There is a post office on the square. The Vatican also has its own license plates which start with SCV. This stands for *Stato dello Città del Vaticano*, or the Vatican city state, but Romans often remark when they see an expensive car with a license plate like that: '*Se Cristo Vedesse*' which means 'If Christ would see..'

2.3 St. Peter's square

On the 17th of February 1655 many people gathered in front of Saint Peter's to await the result of the conclave. Innocent X had died and a conclave had been under way. People started cheering when they saw white smoke emerging from the Sistine Chapel. This was the sign that a new Pope was elected.

Fabio Chigi was elected and chose the name of Alexander VII. This new Pope really wanted to finish Saint Peter's. One thing that still had to be done was to create a beautiful Piazza in front of the church. This was the place where many people gathered for important religious days, like Easter and Christmas.

Bernini got this very important commission from Pope Alexander VII. This Pope really liked commissioning imposing structures and also liked to make an imposing impression wherever he went. Whenever he would go anywhere he would take a thousand soldiers with him.

Bernini created a square which symbolizes the arms of the Church, which welcomes you as you enter the square. We are sort of embraced by the square. You have to imagine coming to Rome after a long pilgrimage. When you finally arrive at the Vatican, the symbolic arms of the church embrace you to welcome you.

The colonnade consists of 4 pillars behind each other. There is one central point on each side of the square, close to the fountains where it looks like there is only one pillar. This point is always easy to find, because lots of people stand on it to look at the pillars. On top of the colonnade there are 96 statues. They represent Saints and other important people in the history of the church. They were all designed by Bernini. If you would like at them from close-by you would see they are not very polished. Bernini knew people would only see them from far. They are completely designed to be looked at from below, at an angle of 45 degrees from below.

By this time, Bernini had many artists working for him. If you look at all the statues on top of the colonnade you can imagine that he did not make all these himself. Bernini was a powerful artist with a big workshop.

2.4 The fountains

Image 3 by Radomil Wikimedia Commons

There are two fountains on the square, made by Bernini and Maderno. The fountain by Maderno was already there when Bernini designed the square. Bernini created another one so there would be symmetry in the square. Maderno is the same artist that also designed the façade of Saint Peter's

2.5 The obelisk

The obelisk in the middle is 25 meters high, made from red granite. It already stood there when Bernini started working on the square. Emperor Caligula ordered it to be erected around here. It came from Egypt, where it was created under the pharaohs. The Romans really liked all things Egyptian. We have to realize that the Egyptian culture was already 2000 years old in the time of Julius Caesar. People like him looked to the ancient Egyptians like we look to the Romans now. The Romans loved the obelisks of Egypt so much, that many of them were taken from Egypt to Rome. Now, there are more obelisks in Rome than in the whole of Egypt.

A special ship was made to transport this one from Egypt to Rome. On the pedestal it says Caligula dedicated it to his predecessors Augustus and Tiberius. It was placed on the square in 1586 during the Papacy of Sixtus V, who was obsessed by obelisks. He had them excavated all over town and resurrected. He had workers go around the city with long metal sticks to poke the earth around places where it was suspected obelisks could be found.

When this one was raised, none of the workers was allowed to speak, because they all had to be able to hear the instructions. The punishment for speaking was death, but when the obelisk was halfway up a sailor screamed 'put water on the ropes'. He was not punished but rewarded because if this had not happened the ropes would have snapped and the obelisk would have fallen down.

2.6 The Apostolic palace

Image 4 Photo by Wknight94 Wikimedia Commons

    The Papal Palaces you can see towering above Saint Peter's Square were built in the late 1500s. Inside, there are 1400 rooms, twenty courtyards, an Olympic sized swimming pool, a bowling alley and a movie theater. The Pope used to live on the third floor and his window is on the top level. It is the second window to the far right. Pope Francis I is not living here. He decided the apartments were too luxurious for him, so he stays in the same room he stayed in when he came to Rome for the conclave as a Cardinal. It's in the simple hotel inside the Vatican that John Paul II had constructed for guests of the Vatican.

    The Pope still does the blessing on Sundays from the window of the Papal Apartments.

2.7 The statues of St. Peter and St. Paul

    In front of the church you can see two statues. They are Saint Peter and Saint Paul. You can recognize Peter by the keys in his hand, because he possesses the keys to heaven. Paul is always recognizable by the sword. This is because he was not crucified, but beheaded by a sword. This was his right as a Roman citizen. Peter and Jesus were not Roman citizens so they were crucified, which is a much more painful death.

2.8 The Balcony

Image 5 by Jean-Pol GRANDMONT Wikimedia Commons

The balcony where the Pope is presented to the people of the world after the conclave is the one above the main door, with the red color on the walls on both sides. It is also from this balcony the Pope blesses the city and the world every Easter, the Urbi et Orbi. Under the balcony there is a carving which shows Jesus handing the keys to heaven to Saint Peter.

2.9 History of St. Peter's basilica

Do you know what this site was before St. Peter's Basilica was built? It was Caligula's Circus, which was later enlarged by Nero. Nero reigned from 54 AD to 68 AD and during his reign there was a great fire in 64 AD. Some historians say Nero had to blame somebody for the fire, because some people said he started it himself to make room for his new Golden Palace, the Domus Aurea. So Nero blamed the Christians, which was considered a new strange sect and told them that the Roman Gods were angry at them for worshiping only one God.

Nero was the first to persecute Christians. Saint Peter died during these persecutions. According to legend, Peter had heard people wanted to arrest him so he left Rome, but just as he had left the city gates and was walking down Via Appia he came across Jesus who was walking the other way. Peter then famously said 'Quo Vadis Domine', where are you going my Lord. Jesus then replied that he was going back to Rome to be crucified again. Peter then knew that his time had come and he had to go back to Rome and die for his faith. He was arrested and then crucified in Nero's Circus. Peter asked to be crucified upside down, because he thought he was not worthy to be crucified the same way as Jesus. If you ever see someone being crucified upside down in a painting, you can be sure it is Saint Peter.

Peter was then buried in a small necropolis next to the circus and over time this became a place for worship for the increasing number of Christians in the city

Then Emperor Constantine decided to become Christian. How and if this really happened is a longer story that I will tell you when I will show you Bernini's statue of him and the enormous fresco in the Room of Constantine inside the Vatican museums.

Constantine ordered the building of Saint Peters Basilica. The building was built on the site of Saint Peters burial place. Construction was started in 324. The Basilica was consecrated in 326.

Of course the building you see today is not that building. Saint Peter's was rebuilt in the 16th century in Renaissance and Baroque styles. It was Pope Julius II who ordered that the old Basilica had to be torn down and a new one be built in 1506. He commissioned the famous renaissance architect Donato Bramante to design a new church. Of course both Julius II and Bramante died during the same decade and so the plan changed quite a few times (some of the architects that were involved were Raphael and Antonio da Sangallo) until in 1546 Michelangelo who was now 70 years old was assigned as the main architect for the Basilica. Michelangelo did not get paid for his work; he did it for the glory of the work and for his own salvation. He died at the age of 88 and work on the dome ceased for 24 years. It was finally finished in 22 months by Giacomo della Porta and Domenico Fontana.

The original plan was for a church with a Greek cross floor plan, instead of a Latin cross, but in 1600 Pope Paul V commissioned Carlo Maderno to change the floor plan into a Latin cross. This way the church became much bigger than originally intended. Carlo Maderno is also responsible for the facade of the church and for the fountain on the right side of the piazza. Bernini added the other fountain to make it more symmetrical. Students of Bernini added the sculptures on top of the facade. You can see Christ in the middle and ten apostles, replacing Judas with John the Baptist

Paulus V added the text on the facade 'In Honorem Principis Apost. - Paulus v Burghesius Romanus Pont. Max. Anno MDCXII - Pont. VII' which translates as: 'In honor of the Prince of Apostles, Pontifex Maximus Paul V of the Borghese family made this in the year 1612'. The letters are two meters high

It took nearly 120 years to build the Church. Most of the material is marble, granite and travertine. Some of the building material came from the Colosseum and Forum, where it was taken from ancient buildings.

2.10 Vatican Museums

Image 6 By Aaron Logan, from
http://www.lightmatter.net/gallery/Italy_Portfolio/vaticanmuseum

    The Vatican museums are fourteen kilometers long and there are about two thousand rooms in the museum. It is said that if you spend sixty seconds looking at every item in the museum you will spend twelve years in here. In this guide I will guide you through the most famous parts of the museum and show you the most important works of art.

    It is important to realize that the spaces you will walk through were never built as a museum. They were the private quarters of the Pope. So the museum is one direction only, just because some passageways are so small

    The founder of the museum was a very important Pope. His name was Julius II. We will meet this Pope many more times during this tour. In 1506 a statue was found on Esquiline hill. Julius sent Michelangelo to examine it and on his recommendation he immediately bought it. He put it on display in the Vatican for all to see. The statue is still there and you will see it later. It is still one of the highlights of the museum. But first, let's visit Saint Peter's Basilica.

3. ST. PETER'S BASILICA

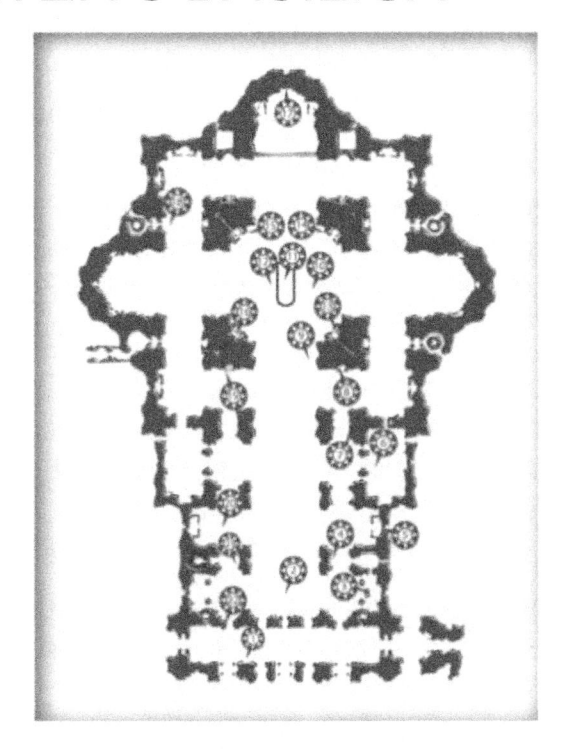

The most important thing to think of when you plan to visit Saint Peter's is to make sure to dress appropriately. If you don't, the guards will not let you in. This means you should cover your shoulders and knees. There are no exceptions. You have to pass a clothing inspection at the entrance, where on a sunny day you will see many scantily dressed girls and older men in shorts that have not been allowed to go in.

There are three main things to see here. You can visit the church itself. Inside the church, there are stairs that lead to a lower level. Here you can see the graves of many popes. You can also decide to visit the cupula. Just follow the signs once you passed the clothing inspection. The view from the top is beautiful, but you do have to pay an entrance fee and on some days the lines are very long here too.

You can confess in the right transept of the church. You can confess in many languages here. If you want to attend mass, it's regularly celebrated in the left transept of the church. You will not be able to light any candles, because it damages the many artworks inside the church. For lighting candles, I recommend a visit to Santa Prassede, a small and beautiful church near Santa Maria Maggiore.

Make sure to take this guidebook to Saint Peter's basilica. Of course there are many other good options. Just take a book or order a tour in advance with one of the recommended tour operators on TripAdvisor.

There are toilets on Saint Peter's Square. They are free. Most people go to the ones that are located on the left side when facing the façade of the church. This is because you exit the church on that side. There are other ones located on the right (northern) side, just under the Papal Apartments. Normally, these ones are much quieter.

Next to the less busy toilets on the north side of Saint Peter's square, you can also find a Vatican post office here, where you can buy Vatican Stamps.

You can decide to use the Vatican postal service to send your cards and letters. You can find a post office on the square, but also inside the Vatican museums. You will have to write you cards here, because you can only post at the Vatican itself. The post boxes outside the Vatican are operated by the Italian state and take only cards and letters with Italians stamps on them. The Vatican post is famous because it works a lot better than the Italian postal service. So take your written cards with you and post them with beautiful Vatican stamps here. Now, let's enter the Basilica!

3.1 Portico

If you enter under the balcony you will first end up in a hall. Here, on the far left and right sides you can see two statues. On the left side you can see a statue of Charlemagne, who was crowned by the Pope inside the church in the year 800, which was a very important moment in church history. Popes could crown Emperors!

On the right side is a more beautiful statue, made by Bernini. It is Constantine, the first Christian Emperor and the founder of the first Saint Peter's Basilica.

Figure 1 Equestrian Statue of Emperor Constantine, 1670

Constantine was one the most important figures in western history. He was the first Emperor that became Christian. Historians are not quite sure if he ever was baptized. Most people believe he was baptized just before dying, because the Emperor thought it was impossible to be a good Christian and a good Emperor at the same time. This is the last monument built in classical Rome, because Emperor Constantine soon moved the capital to a new city on the Bosporus, which came to be known as Constantinople, now Istanbul.

Constantine became Christian because the day before an important battle he had a dream in which he saw a cross. An angel then told him 'In hoc signo vinces' or 'In this sign you will conquer'. The next day Constantine ordered all his soldiers to paint crosses on their shield and of course he won the battle and became the sole Emperor. Afterwards he started sponsoring Christianity.

He ordered the building of Saint Peter's Basilica and Saint John of Lateran. He also presided over Church councils, like the one in Milan, in which Christianity was legalized. Constantine's influence was enormous. Historians estimate that before Constantine about 5% of the population of the empire was Christian, after Constantine about 60 to 70% of the population was Christian.

Bernini depicts Constantine while he is having his vision, just before the battle of the Milvian Bridge. He is riding his horse, and suddenly he sees a vision of a cross in the sky. The horse even seems to see the cross, because it jumps with his front legs in the air. Constantine fixes his eyes on the cross, which is illuminating in the heavens.

Bernini's usual tricks are very much present in this statue. There is a small window, which you can't even see, that brings light to Constantine's face, just like with Longinus.

This way of sculpting an equestrian statue was completely new. Before, kings and rulers were always shown to sit quietly on a horse, symbolizing the control they had over their kingdom. Here, the horse is wild. It jumps up. No one had ever sculpted like that and this statue was very influential on later artists.

Again, we see the characteristics of Bernini's Baroque art. Bernini sculpts a dramatic moment. Something important is happening. Furthermore, the statue is fixed on something which is not sculpted, in this case the cross. The cross exists in our space, the space of the spectator. In this way, we are drawn to the statue. Also, Bernini is very skillfully sculpting fabric. In this case, the marble cloth that you can see behind Constantine also supports the whole statue.

The main doors in the middle comes from the old basilica. Inside there are 44 altars, 11 domes, 778 columns, 135 mosaic paintings and 395 statues. The church is 192 meters long. It is the largest church in the world and they have markings to prove it. In the middle of the church the names and lengths of other churches can be seen. This is why the middle section is blocked, so that people stop walking over the markings.

The doors on the right are the Holy Doors. They are opened only every 25 years in a Jubilee year, a Holy year. The next Holy year was supposed to be in 2025, but Pope Francis proclaimed a special Holy year for 2016. This is highly unusual.

If you look at the Holy Door from the inside you will see the entrance is closed with bricks. This tradition was started by Alexander VI, the Borgia Pope. The last time they were opened was in the year 2000 by Pope John Paul II. They are made of bronze. The opening of the doors always takes place on Christmas Eve. The Pope knocks on the doors with a silver hammer and they open up. He is first to go through and followed by the rest of clergy and pilgrims. This happens in all the mayor Basilica's of Rome. Santa Maria Maggiore, Saint John Lateran and Saint Paul outside the walls all have holy doors. They symbolize the entrance to heaven and if you pass through your sins are supposedly forgiven. After the Holy year the doors are closed with bricks again.

3.2 Porphyry circle

Enter the main door go straight to the left where you will see a red circle on the floor. The circle is made of porphyry, the same expensive stone you will see a lot in the Vatican Museums. For example, Nero's bathtub in the Vatican museums is made of this material. On this spot, but a few meters below, Charlemagne was crowned Emperor of the Holy Roman Empire by the Pope on Christmas Eve in the year 800 in the old Saint Peter's (whose floor level was lower than the current church. Mother Teresa, Queen Elizabeth, Lady Diana and even George Clooney have all stood on this circle.

3.3 La Pietà

Image 7 by Stanislav Traykov Wikimedia Commons

This statue is one of the most famous in the world. It is the Pietà by Michelangelo. Pietà means pity or sorrow. Michelangelo was only 23 years old and it took him one year to sculpt. It is the only artwork by the artist that is signed. If you look at the ribbon across Maria's chest you can see his name. It says *Michelangelo Buanorotte Florentino ha fatto questo*, Michelangelo Buonarotti from Florence has made this.

According to legend, he signed this work, because one day he was looking at his statue and some people came in and said the statue was made by a different sculptor. Michelangelo got angry and chiseled his name in at night.

Michelangelo has been criticized for this work as well. Critics say that if Maria would stand up, she would be twice as big as Christ. Also, some considered Maria to be way too youthful. She looks younger than her son. The reason Maria looks big, is because nowadays the statue stands in the wrong position. Michelangelo created it thinking it would stand on ground level. So you would look at the statue from above. If you look at the statue like that, suddenly the perspective works. The same applies to the David in Florence. People criticize this statue because its hands, feet and head are too big for its body. This is because the statue was meant to stand on the Cathedral, far up. People would only be able to see it from far, so he made the hands and feet bigger so you can notice them. Michelangelo always knew where his statues were supposed to stand and sculpted them with this position in mind. After, often his statues were moved and can seem a little bit out of perspective. This is not the artists fault though.

In 1972 a disturbed person entered the church and screamed "I am Jesus and this is not my mother". He destroyed some parts of the statue with a hammer and broke her nose. Some tourists took pieces with them as a souvenir. The man was arrested and put in the Vatican jail cell, the last person to have been in a Vatican jail. Ever since security is very strict. The statue is now behind bulletproof glass, which is a shame, because you cannot see it from up close and see the beautiful expressions on the faces of Mary and Jesus.

3.4 Christina of Sweden

Image 8 by Torvindus.Wikimedia Commons

A little bit further you can see the monument in honor of Christina of Sweden. She was a protestant queen who became

Catholic. Because Sweden was a protestant nation she had to give up her throne. She moved to Rome when she was 29 years old in 1655 and was welcomed as a hero. Her conversion had been very good Propaganda for the Catholic Church at the time. This is the reason she had to honor to be buried inside Saint Peter's. It seems she was quite a character and caused many problems for the Pope. She used to wear men's clothes and was only 1.50 meters high. People say the love of her life was a cardinal in Rome, Azzolino.

3.5 The grave of John Paul II

Image 9 by Wojciech Pawlik Wikimedia Commons

Following the church on the right side you can see something relatively new. The body of Pope John Paul II was transferred here recently after he was blessed. John Paul II was Pope from 1978 until 2005. He now is one of the few popes that are buried inside the Basilica and not in the crypts below. Because of his continuing popularity, you will see many people praying in front of his tomb.

3.6 Chapel of the Holy Sacrament

After passing John Paul II's grave, you will see the Chapel of the Holy Sacrament on your right. This is the only place in the Basilica where you can pray in silence. Inside you are not allowed to take pictures. The altar inside was designed by Gian Lorenzo Bernini, the famous baroque sculptor.

3.7 The monument for Pope Gregory XIII

This simple monument is for Gregory XIII. He is the Pope who commissioned the Gallery of the Maps inside the Vatican Museums. He founded the Astrology department at the Vatican and is still famous for giving us the Gregorian calendar, the calendar we still use today. Before this we used the Julian Calendar, which Julius Caesar had introduced. This calendar was wrong, because every year was 11 minutes too short, so after a lot of years, the calendar was evidently wrong. Gregory had a team of specialists create a new, correct calendar, one that we still use today.

3.8 The grave of John XXIII

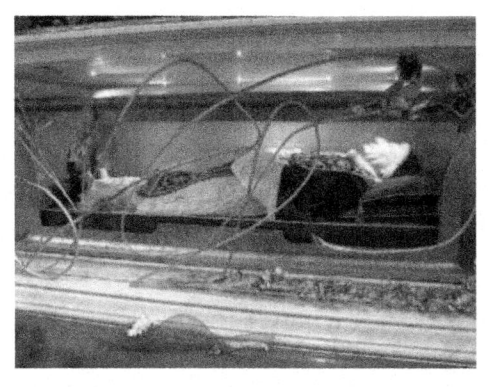

Image 10 by Dnalor 01 1CC BY-SA 3.0 Wikimedia Commons

There are a few Popes buried on this level of the church. The other 147 are buried below in the crypt, which you can visit, and also see through the openings in the floor on this level. Besides John Paul II, the most famous Pope that is buried in the church itself is John XXIII, who died 1963. Soon after, it was found out that his body was not decomposing. This was seen as a miracle. You can see him in a glass coffin, covered in wax. This Pope was very famous because of the very important Church Council that took place during his Papacy, Vatican II.

3.9 Statue of St Peter

Everybody comes to this statue in the middle of the church to touch the right foot of Saint Peter. It is said that if you do this you will be blessed. This statue came from the old Saint Peter's and was made by Arnolfo di Cambio around 1300. You can see Peter's foot has almost disappeared from all the touching. Every year, on the feast day of Saint Peter and Paul, the statue is dressed up in Papal robes. The Catholic Church considers Saint Peter to be the first Pope. According to Canonic Law, every Pope succeeds Saint Peter, not his direct predecessor.

3.10 The Dome

Image 11 by Attila Terbócs Wikimedia Commons

If you look up you can see Michelangelo's dome. It is a beautiful piece of architecture. It was his idea to make a dome like the Pantheon's, but lift it up on pillars, and that is exactly what we see. He himself thought the dome of his native Florence was more beautiful and he made the diameter of his dome half a meter shorter than that of the Pantheon, in honor of the unknown architect of that building. The words around the dome say in Latin 'Tu es Petrus et super hanc petram aedificabo ecclesiam meam et tibi dabo claves regni caelorum': You are Peter and upon this rock I will build My Church and I will give you the keys to heaven', the famous sentence Jesus said and on which the Popes base their authority as successors of Saint Peter, who is considered the first Pope. The dome weighs 56 million kilograms and is 136.5 meter high, which is 447.8 feet. You can climb the dome. The entrance is outside the Church on the right side, looking from the square.

3.11 The Papal altar

Under the dome we can see the *confessio* and the Papal altar. The *confessio* is where Saint Peter is buried. You cannot see his grave from here, but it is supposed to be behind the niche in the back, right under the dome. The Pallium is kept here. This is a circular band of white wool which the Pope places on the shoulders of each newly appointed Archbishop on June 29, the feast of Saint Peter and Paul. The wool comes from sheep that are blessed by the Pope on the day of Saint Agnes. Above is the Papal Altar, which only the Pope may use. It is one piece of marble that came from Roman times. From here, the Pope says mass only twice a year, on Christmas and Easter. These oil candles are always lit in honor of St Peter.

3.12 The Baldacchino

The Baldacchino is the four-legged structure above the Papal altar in Saint Peter's. When Bernini got the commission, Saint Peter's was just finished. The church was consecrated in 1626, but it still had to be decorated inside. One of the most important decorations would be the ornamentations of the Papal altar, above the grave of Saint Peter. Bernini got the commission to create this.

He started in the same year Saint Peter's was consecrated. Of course, there had been a Saint Peter's since the time of Emperor Constantine in the third century ad. But at the beginning of the sixteenth century, Pope Julius II had torn down the old early medieval Saint Peter's and started working on a new one, which was now finished.

The Baldacchino was a big commission. It was something else than carving a man-sized statue for a Cardinal or Nobleman. The Baldacchino would mix architecture with art. It had to be done in bronze, not stone. Bronze is much harder to work with. The procedure of creating a bronze statue is very difficult, let alone a much bigger structure like the Baldacchino.

Bernini started with a wooden model. Then he created two life-sized columns from wood. After this the wood was recreated in clay and wax. All of this Bernini could not do alone of course. By this time, Bernini had a big workshop where he employed many men.

After he created the wax model, Bernini had a problem. Where could he get that amount of bronze? Bronze was expensive and there was not enough money in the budget to buy it. Where could they get all this bronze? What do you think? Where did they get it?

Of course, as so often happened in this time, the bronze was taken from an ancient Roman building.

This is the Pantheon in Rome. It was built in 27 bc and rebuilt by Emperor Hadrian (of the wall) in the second century after Christ. Nowadays, it is, according to me, the most impressive Roman building still standing, surpassing even the Colosseum in beauty.

The building was once a temple to all the gods. It had a Greek name. 'Pan' means 'all' and 'theon' means gods. The pantheon is still standing, because in 609 it was given to the Pope by the East-Roman Emperor Phocas. The Pope then made it into a church, which is why the building is still standing. He called it 'Santa

Maria ad Martyres' and had 28 carts with bones of martyrs brought here from the catacombs to be buried.

In Bernini's time, the roof of the portico was still covered with enormous bronze plates.

In 1632 Pope Urban VIII of the Barberini family took the bronze beams from the front porch and melted them down to give to Bernini for the Baldacchino in Saint Peter's Basilica. He stole about 250.000 kilos of bronze. He had enough bronze left to also make 40 canons for the Castel Sant'Angelo.

After this the Roman people said:

'Quod non fecerunt barbari, Barberini fecerunt'; what the barbarians didn't do, the Barberinis did.

According to legend, the first time this was said, it was said to the Pope himself.

Even now, almost 2000 years after it was built, the Pantheon is still used as a place of worship. The marble interior is mostly original.

Pope Urban VIII was not the first to take building material from ancient monuments. Half of the Colosseum was torn down to build Palazzo Farnese in Rome for Pope Paul V. Many of the early medieval churches in Rome use columns that were taken from ancient temples and buildings. If you are ever in Rome in a medieval church, have a look at the columns. You can often see that they are not the same at all. Sometimes they are not even the same height.

Now, Bernini had enough bronze to complete his Baldacchino.

The columns were created from bronze and then ornamented with real gold. This was not the most expensive material that was used on the Baldacchino though. Strangely enough, some art historians have checked the accountant's books, and found out the most expensive material that was used to create this enormous artwork was the high quality bee's wax.

The columns of the Baldacchino are twisted. This is a reference to the column against which Jesus was whipped. Traditionally, this column is depicted twisted in painting. The columns refer to the suffering of Christ.

Other decorations are laurel leaves and bees. The bees return everywhere on the Baldacchino. This is because Urban VIII's coat of arms included three bees. It is the coat of arms of the Barberini family.

The Baldacchino symbolizes heaven. Besides the fact that they stole the bronze from the Pantheon, the choice of bronze is a good one. It really fits with the colors of the interior of the church. It is a slender structure, which leaves enough space to look right through it to the other side. This is important, because if you enter the church and look ahead, you would need to see the Basilica's apsis. In the apsis, the seat of Saint Peter is located. So it was very important that Bernini left the view of this seat open. Later, Bernini would also get the commission to create an artwork to surround this seat. We will talk about this Cathedra Petri later.

3.13 St. Longinus

It was decided there should be balconies in the main columns that supported the dome of Saint Peter's. Inside these columns, some of the most important relics of the church were kept. These relics had to be shown to the people on special religious days. So it was decided there had to be balconies to display these relics.

What were these relics? There was the cloth that Saint Veronica had used to wipe the face of Christ when he was carrying the cross. Then there was the point of the spear that was used to pierce the side of Jesus when he was hanging on the cross. The church also had a piece of the true cross and the head of Saint Andrew, Peter's brother.

Bernini designed the balconies and the bas-reliefs above them. Under the balconies, Bernini made space for four important statues, one of Saint Andrew, one of Saint Veronica, one of Saint Helen (Emperor Constantine's mother, who brought the cross back from Jerusalem) and one statue of Saint Longinus.

This statue of Saint Longinus Bernini made himself. Who was this Longinus? He was the soldier that used his lance to pierce the side of Christ while he was on the cross. You might ask, why was this Roman soldier later canonized?

This is because Longinus immediately realized what he had done. As soon as he pierced Christ, he received Godly inspiration and called out: 'This is truly God's son'. He then converted and was later martyred. His name comes from the Greek word for lance.

Longinus did not try to hurt Christ when he pierced his side. People who were crucified could await a very long and painful death. Mercy could be shown by piercing the side of a convict, so he would quickly bleed out and not have to suffer long.

Bernini depicts Longinus here just after he pierced Christ. He is right in the moment of understanding who this man on the cross is. It seems a light beam comes from above and illuminates him. In the church, this is actually the case. Light comes from above, from the windows in the cupula, something Bernini was very much aware of when he made this statue.

We see the main characteristics of the art of Bernini in this work. One: he depicts the moment of action. Longinus is in the moment of receiving a Godly message. Two: Just like with the statue of David, the statue is focused on something outside, in this case the Godly light. Three: the statue is experiencing a very strong emotion. He is converted in this moment and afterwards his faith will be so strong that he is willing to die for it.

Another typical Baroque characteristic is the use of the cloth that envelops his body. Look at how it flows and how light it seems, even though it is made of marble.

Also, have a look at the spear of Longinus. This is also part of the statue, which was made out of one piece of marble. You cannot be unimpressed by the great skill of Bernini when you see this.

3.14 St. Helena

The second statue is Saint Helena; she was Emperor Constantine's mother and a devout catholic. She went on a pilgrimage to Jerusalem to retrieve the Cross on which Christ was crucified. She brought it back to Rome and pieces of it are kept inside the pillar.

3.15 St. Veronica

The third statue represents Saint Veronica. She saw Christ fall for the third time when he was carrying his cross up the hill and stepped forward to wipe his face with her veil. An image of Christ's face remained on the fabric. We do not know her real name, but she was named Veronica, because *Vero* means true and *Nica* means icon in Greek, so her name means true icon.

3.16 St. Andrew

The last statue is Saint Andrew, Patron Saint of Scotland and Greece. He was Peter's brother and went to Greece to spread the Christian faith. He cured the Roman Governor's wife of a serious illness and converted her to Christianity, but it is said that he persuaded her to also deny her husband his marital rights, which is what got him beheaded, not his preaching. The head however is no longer here, a treaty was signed in 1966 with the Greek Orthodox Church and as a token of good will the head was sent back to Greece.

3.17 Cathedra Petri

Image 12 by Vitold Muratov CC BY-SA 3.0 Wiki Commons

This monument, at the back of the Church was also made by Gian Lorenzo Bernini. *Cathedra Petri* is Latin for the Seat of Peter. This seat had been in Saint Peter's since the ninth century. It had always stood in the old Saint Peter's that was built under Emperor Constantine. This seat was too important to be discarded, so it had to find a new home inside the new Saint Peter's.

According to tradition, this was the seat of Saint Peter, who is considered to be the first Pope. Research from the 1960s has shown that the seat was not from the time of Saint Peter, but from the ninth century. It probably belonged to an early French king.

However, the seat is an important symbol. The seat of Saint Peter is a symbol for the Papacy. The Pope is the direct successor of Saint Peter and the guardian of the church on earth.

It was decided the seat had to move to the apsis, where it would get a more prominent place. Bernini then created this enormous artwork. It is a mix between architecture and sculpture. He used different colors of marble, gilded bronze, stucco, bas-reliefs and sculptures.

To give you an idea of the dimensions, the wingspan of the dove is almost two meters or a little over six feet. The windows are made of alabaster. This is a stone which you would get if you compressed marble for millions of years. It has an interesting quality. It lets light through, which is why it was used here. It represents the light of the Holy Spirit. Next to the alabaster windows you can see small figures that become bigger the further they get from the window. Bernini wants to say here that all beings originate from the light of God.

Below you can see the seat of Saint Peter. It is being held up by four Church fathers. This artwork became very influential and many artists have imitated it. One of the most famous imitations can be found on the ceiling of the Gesù church in Rome, the same church Bernini visited every day.

3.18 The funerary monument to Alexander VII

Image 13 by Jean-Pol GRANDMONT CC BY 3.0 Wikimedia commons

This beautiful and extravagant monument was finished by Bernini when he was very old, at the age of 80. He did work on it himself, with the help of his students.

When Bernini got the commission he had one problem. There was a door in the place the monument was supposed to stand. So

Bernini, very cleverly, used the door in his composition. How did he do it? You can see a skeleton coming from under the big cloth, with his hands up. In his hands he holds an hourglass, saying Alexander's time has come. The cloth represents the cloth of death which covers everything and the door of course symbolizes the passage to the next life.

There are also the female figures which represent the four virtues of the Pope: Justice, Prudence, Charity and Truth. Take a good look at Truth; she has her foot over a globe. Bernini decided to make Italy very big, because Rome of course was the center of the world. Under Truth's big toe you can see a horn coming from England. This refers to the problem the Church had with Henry VIII, who wanted a divorce from his wife which the Pope refused to grant. Henry then decided to form his own Church.

Look at the enormous marble cloth.

It is amazing how light it looks. It is really made of marble and very heavy. The cloth symbolizes a funerary shroud. Under the shroud you can see Death appear in the form of a skeleton.

3.19 The Transfiguration by Raphael

This is a copy of a painting that now hangs inside the Vatican Museum. This is a mosaic; if you look closely you can see it is made out of a lot of tiny stones. The painting was Raphael's last work; he was very ill when he painted it and knew he was dying. He asked his friends to carry this painting to the Pantheon on the day of his funeral, because he loved this painting so much. It is indeed one of his masterpieces. If you have the time, go and see it as well in the Pinacoteca of the Vatican Museums, because the real thing is much more impressive.

It of course represents the Transfiguration. This is when Christ showed his true godly nature to Saint John, Saint Peter and Saint James. He starts flying and Elijah and Moses appear next to him in the sky. The apostles fall down, blinded by the light.

Below all those people are in a state of confusion. Some apostles are trying to cure a possessed boy, which they cannot do. Only the transfigured Christ, later, will save the boy.

Raphael's love of his life was a baker's daughter. He was never allowed to marry her, because she was too poor. In Italian she is called *La Fornarina*. She appears in many of his paintings. Here we see her in pink and blue on the foreground. When Raphael died she entered a monastery.

3.20 The coat-of-arms of John Paul II

Image 14 by User:mAgul Wikimedia Commons

If you look to the floor you can see the coat-of-arms of John Paul II. He designed this himself. Before, Popes were of noble decent and so had a coat-of-arms. The modern popes are no longer from the nobility so they design their own coat-of-arms. John Paul used the colors of the Vatican flag, the M for Mary, because he dedicated his papacy to the Virgin Mary, who always had inspired him. Then you can see the words Totus Tuus means totally yours. PM stands for Pontifex Maximus, an old Roman title for the highest priest which the Popes took over.

3.21 The monument to James III

James III was the last of the Stuarts, the family that ruled England for many years. This monument is made by Antonio Canova, the same artist that did Perseus with the head of Medusa in the Vatican museums. This family was expelled from England, because they did not want to give up their Catholic faith. They took refuge in Rome 1689. His wife also got a monument in front of him. This is a neo-classical artwork, which makes it stand out in the church, because most of the interior is Baroque.

3.22 Exit

Now make sure not to exit to the door on the far right. This supposedly brings bad luck, because through that door coffins would exit after a funerary service.

4. VATICAN MUSEUMS 1: ENTRANCE

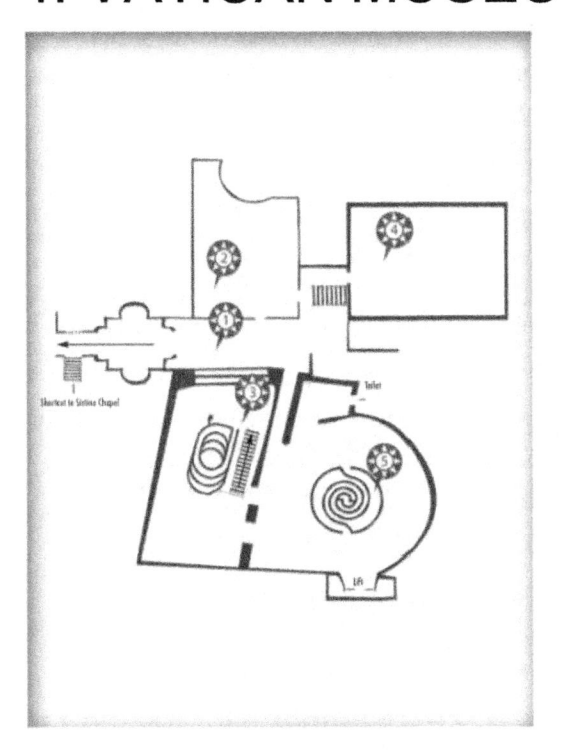

4.1 Entering the museums

Make sure to book a ticket online before trying to enter the museums. If you don't you risk standing in line for a very long time. Also make sure to book it through the official site of the Vatican: www.vatican.va.

Pay attention not to take any sharp object with you. You will not be allowed to enter. Everybody has to go through security to enter the museums, which is much like passing security in an airport. If you have a big backpack, the guards will sometimes make you deposit it in the *guardaroba*.

After you passed security you move up the stairs where you will obtain your physical ticket. With this ticket you can then enter the museums. After you showed your ticket, you will go up a very long escalator. You can see this escalator at number 3 in the map above. You can also walk up the very long walkway that takes you to the same place. There are also elevators available.

Once you arrive at the top of the escalators, you have a few options. Remember that most of the museum is one direction only. You cannot move freely through the halls. If you go to the left, you will begin making you way towards the Sistine Chapel. To the right, you can find the Pinacoteca (the painting collection of the Vatican) and the restaurants and coffee bars. You can also go straight and go outside to the little courtyard. I'd advise you to do this first, because you have a very beautiful view of the dome of Saint Peter's. This courtyard is at number 2 on my map. 4 is the Pinacoteca.

Once you have finished your tour through the museum, you will end up back here, unless you took the door to Saint Peter's inside the Sistine Chapel (there are two exits in the Chapel, make sure you know which one you want to take). Number 5 on my map represents the big round staircase that takes you to the exit.

When I talk about the Sistine Chapel and Michelangelo's work at the Vatican, I always like to start with a quote from Mark Twain, from his book 'Innocents abroad'.

'In this connection I wish to say one word about Michelangelo Buonarroti. I used to worship the mighty genius of Michelangelo-- that man who was great in poetry, painting, sculpture, architecture-- great in everything he undertook. But I do not want Michelangelo for breakfast-- for luncheon -- for dinner--for tea--for supper--for between meals. I like a change, occasionally. In Genoa, he designed everything; in Milan he or his pupils designed everything; he designed the Lake of Como; in Padua, Verona, Venice, Bologna, who did we ever hear of, from guides, but Michael Angelo? In

Florence, he painted everything, designed everything, nearly, and what he did not design he used to sit on a favorite stone and look at, and they showed us the stone. In Pisa he designed everything but the old shot-tower, and they would have attributed that to him if it had not been so awfully out of the perpendicular. He designed the piers of Leghorn and the custom house regulations of Civita Vecchia. But, here--here it is frightful. He designed St. Peter's; he designed the Pope; he designed the Pantheon, the uniform of the Pope's soldiers, the Tiber, the Vatican, the Colosseum, the Capitol, the Tarpeian Rock, the Barberini Palace, St. John Lateran, the Campagna, the Appian Way, the Seven Hills, the Baths of Caracalla, the Claudian Aqueduct, the Cloaca Maxima--the eternal bore designed the Eternal City, and unless all men and books do lie, he painted everything in it!

I never felt so fervently thankful, so soothed, so tranquil, so filled with a blessed peace, as I did yesterday when I learned that Michelangelo was dead.'

4.2 Introduction to the Museums

This museum is enormous. The halls are 14 kilometers long and there are about 2000 rooms in the museum. I said before that if you spend sixty seconds looking at every item in the museum you will spend twelve years in here. It is important to realize that the spaces you will walk through were never built as a museum. They were the private quarters of the Pope. So the museum is one direction only, just because some passageways are so small. Sometimes you will feel like a pack of sheep driven towards the same destination. There is not much to do about this. It is very important to stay calm and just undergo everything, especially on a very busy, very warm day.

Like I explained before, the founder of the museum was a very important Pope, Julius II. You have met him before. He was the one that decided to build a new Saint Peter's Basilica. In 1506 a statue was found on Esquiline hill. Julius sent Michelangelo to examine it and on his recommendation he immediately bought it. He put it on display in the Vatican for all to see. The statue is still there and you will see it later. It is still one of the highlights of the museum.

4.3 The entrance

The entrance is a new part of the museum. John Paul II created this new entrance because the old entrance was not suitable to accommodate all the tourists. On average 15,000 people enter the museums. Also, since an attack on the Pietà, the famous statue by Michelangelo in Saint Peter's, security had to be improved. So that is one of the reasons you had to pass security at the entrance.

When you arrive at the top of the escalators, the main museum is up the small stairs and to your left, but first go straight into the little courtyard where you have an amazing view of the dome of Saint Peter's, a design by Michelangelo. Even though Michelangelo considered himself to be a sculptor, he had the capacity to become amazingly good at something in a very short time. So it was only later in his long life that Michelangelo started with architecture. Michelangelo re-designed the dome in 1547, when he was 72 years old (He died when he was 88 years old), and came up with this amazing design. It is the tallest dome in the world with a height of 136.57 meters, which is about 488 feet. Its diameter is just a little bit shorter than that of the Pantheon, because Michelangelo wanted to honor the unknown ancient architect of that building. It is also a bit smaller than the dome in Florence in honor of the architect Filippo Brunelleschi, who was the first man who managed to build an enormous dome, something which no architect had managed since classical times. Michelangelo said himself that although his dome was higher, the one in Florence was more beautiful.

4.4 The Pinacoteca

You can decide to visit the painting collection of the Vatican, the Pinacoteca. This building was specially built in 1932 to house this collection. Compared to the other sections in the museum, it is not very large. My favorite painting here is the Transfiguration of Raphael. I talked a bit about this painting before, when we were in Saint Peter's Basilica. Inside the Basilica there is a mosaic of this painting. The real thing is much more beautiful, so make sure to check it out if you have the time. Many tourists decide to skip the Pinacoteca because it is not on the way to the Sistine Chapel. If you are not an art historian, I advise a quick walkthrough, stopping at some of the paintings you like. Besides the Raphael, you can find a beautiful Caravaggio (The Deposition from the Cross) and an unfinished painting by Leonardo of Saint Jerome. Also check out the Lament over the dead Christ by Venetian artist Giovanni Bellini, one of my favorite painters.

5. THE VATICAN MUSEUMS 2: CORTILE DELLA PIGNA

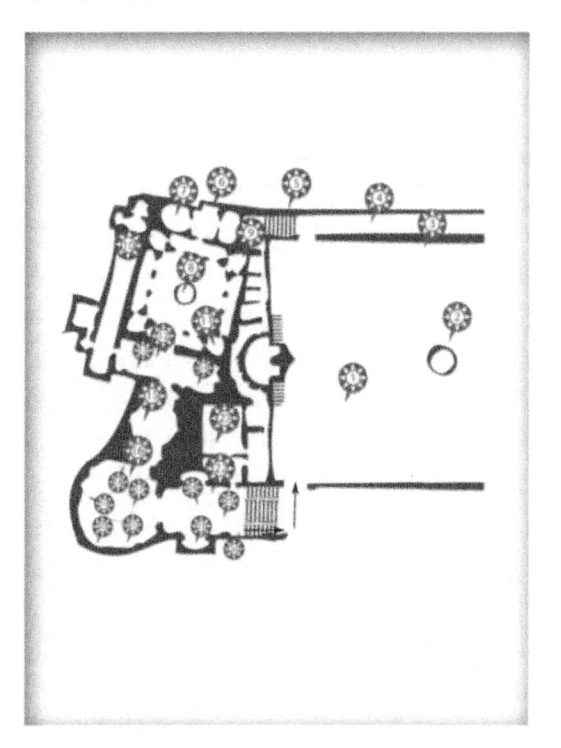

5.1 Cortile della Pigna

Image 15 by Lapula CC BY-SA 3.0 Wikimedia Commons

The first courtyard you enter on your way to the Sistine Chapel is the *Cortile della Pigna.* It is of course named after that big bronze pine cone that used to stand somewhere in the medieval city before it was moved here. It dates back the second century AD and was used as a water fountain (see the difference in color on the top). The base below it came from the ancient Roman baths of Septimus Severus and dates back to the second century AD as well.

The two peacocks on the sides came from Hadrian's Villa in Tivoli (a very nice place for a day trip). They also date back to the second century. Peacocks always represent immortality in ancient art, because it was believed that the flesh from the peacock did not rot after death. This courtyard was used for parties and receptions. In the time of the Borgia Pope Alexander VI bullfights were held here. Alexander came from Spain. Also, once an Elephant lived here as well, who came to the Vatican as a gift to the Pope.

5.2 The globe

In the middle of the courtyard you can see a big bronze globe. It was a gift to John Paul II in 1990 from a famous modern Italian artist named Arnaldo Pomodoro. It has two spheres. It is said it represents the Vatican as its own world inside the rest of the world.

Both spheres were able to move, but the inside one now is broken and is stuck. It cannot be fixed without destroying the whole piece of art.

5.3 The head of Emperor Augustus

Another thing people always notice instantly in the courtyard is the enormous head. This is the head of an ancient statue of the first emperor Augustus. Can you see its hair? The hair was added in the 17th century. This was often done in those times. If a statue was found missing something a Pope would just hired an artist to complete it. So in this museum you can often see an ancient statue with a new nose or new hairdo. This one is a bit extreme because this hair is obviously nothing like Augustus' hair, which we know from other, complete, statues of Augustus.

5.4 Ancient statues

Image 16 by Jean-Pol GRANDMONT CC BY-SA 3.0 Wikimedia Commons

When you cross the courtyard and enter the museums on the other side, you will see a huge collection of ancient busts and statues on your right. These busts are mostly of emperors, senators and gods. They were all found around Rome and were heavily restored. You can walk through the gallery to have a look if you want, but the most important statues are located to your left, up the stairs.

5.5 Frescos next to the stairs

When you walk up the stairs to the left of the entrance, notice the fresco painting on the wall. This style of painting has a very famous name. This style became popular at the end of the 15th century. Around this time, some strange caves were discovered in Rome, decorated with beautiful frescos. It later turned out that the caves once were Emperor Nero's golden house. The style of wall decoration found in the caves became very popular and the style became known as Grotesque, from the Italian grotto for cave.

5.6 The view

On top of the stairs you will see a basin and if you look to your right out the window you will have a nice view of Rome. From here you can see the dome of the Pantheon if you look closely and further away you can see the mountains of the Castelli Romani where the pope has his summer residence in Castel Gandolfo. The palace there is also Vatican territory and also a nice destination for a (half) day trip. If you take the train from Termini station, it takes not too long to arrive at Castelgandolfo. When there, make sure to have a nice lunch as this area is famous for its food. Try the *porchetta* (slow roasted pork, eaten cold) the Frascati wine, the *pecorino* cheese and the olives. Another easy destination in this area is the town of Frascati itself, where you can have a beautiful outdoor dinner, overlooking Rome in the distance. It's also a short train ride from Termini station.

5.7 Apoxyomenos

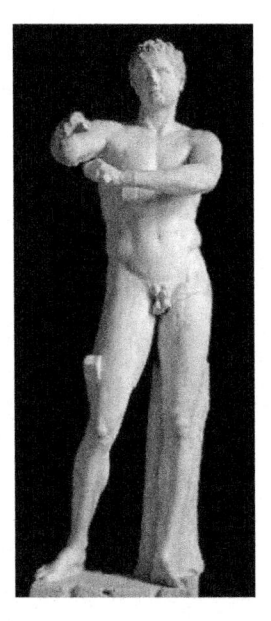

At the end of this space you can see a statue. This is the Apoxyomenos. It is a roman copy of a very famous lost statue by the Greek sculptor Lysippos. Often we only have roman marble copies of Greek statues left, because the bronze statues were often melted down to make things like cannonballs. This artist worked at the court of Alexander the Great. The fun thing about this statue is that it explains nicely how an athlete would clean himself after a wrestling match. In ancient time wrestlers would often put oil all over their body as a form of protection and to make them slippery. After the match the athlete would use an artifact to scrape of the oil and sweat from his body. This is a very good way to clean yourself as the oil extracts all the dirt and sweat from your pores. Romans used this method as well in the bath-houses to clean themselves. A friend or slave would rub you in with oil and then you would scrape it off. This way you get much cleaner than just taking a shower.

5.8 Octagonal courtyard

Image 17 by Manfred Heyde CC BY-SA 3.0 Wikimedia commons

    This is the Octagonal courtyard. It was here where the Vatican Museums started. Julius II put the statue of the Laocoön and other ancient statues that he bought here for the public to see. The courtyard was transformed into an octagonal space in the 1700's by architect Michelangelo Simonetti.

    In this courtyard artists like Michelangelo, Raphael and Bernini sat down and studied the ancient sculptures. You must realize that at that time there were not so many known ancient sculptures. The Vatican collection was nothing like it is today. It was only later that most of the statues you have seen and will see were discovered. So the famous statues Michelangelo and Bernini studied were all found here. This is not just a story, we can see the face of one of the statues here return in some of the most famous works of Michelangelo and Bernini.

    Besides the statues you can see a lot of sarcophagi and bathtubs from ancient times. The bathtubs are made of marble or granite because these materials keep cool and in the summer it is very hot in Rome. You can feel them and notice how cool the rock is. They were brought here from ancient Roman baths around Rome. It is not known to whom the sarcophagi belonged to.

5.9 The Apollo Belvedere

This is a very important statue in this courtyard. Many renaissance and baroque artists used this statue in their own work. Look at the face of Apollo. Later when you will be in the Sistine chapel you will see this face again. Michelangelo copied this face to use for his Jesus figure in his fresco of the last judgment. Look closely so you will remember. He thought the face was one of perfect male beauty.

The statue is called Apollo Belvedere. Apollo was the sun-god and the god of reason and arts. He was second only to Zeus. In one hand he has a bow and the other an arrow, because the romans believed that if a person suddenly died, he was struck down by one of Apollo's arrows. This was a way they could explain heart attacks.

This statue dates back to the second century AD, but it is a copy of a lost Greek bronze from the fourth century BC. It is roman made. We can see this because the roman sculptors were not as good as the Greek. This one needs a little tree trunk to keep standing.

This statue was taken by Napoleon to Paris in 1797 and later returned in 1815 after the battle of the Waterloo. Gian Lorenzo Bernini was also inspired by this statue and used it in his Apollo and Daphne, the amazing statue that is now in the Galleria Borghese. If you have a chance, go see it there. Remember to book your ticket months in advance though as the museum is often fully booked for the weeks ahead.

5.10 Perseus with the head of medusa

Image 18 CC BY-SA 3.0 Wikimedia Commons

This statue is a neo-classical piece by Antonio Canova made in the 1800's. When Napoleon conquered Italy his troops stole the famous ancient statues (like the Apollo Belvedere) from the octagonal courtyard and took them to Paris. To replace them, this statue was put here. It is a masterpiece by Antonio Canova. It represents the story of the medusa. The medusa was a monster. She was a woman with snakes for hair. If you would look into her eyes you would turn into stone. Many warriors and heroes had come and tried to kill her but all had been turned into stone. Then came the Greek hero Perseus. He was smart. He never looked for medusa but instead looked into the reflection of his sword. This way he could see where she was and like this he managed to cut off her head.

The boxers in front of them are Kreugas and Damoxenos, also by Antonio Canova. During a match Damoxenos stabbed Kreugas and pulled out his intestines so he was automatically disqualified and the dead Kreugas was named the winner.

After Napoleon was defeated Antonio Canova was sent to Paris as an ambassador to try to get the stolen statues back. He managed to get them back and as a reward his own statue was allowed to remain in the octagonal courtyard which was an enormous honor.

5.11 Laocoön Group

The most important statue here is the Laocoön Group. It dates back to the first century AD, but the original Greek bronze dated back to the second century BC. The original is lost, like so many original bronze Greek statues. It is called a monolithic statue, because it is made from one single block of marble. It was sculpted by three artists from Rhodes.

It represents a Trojan Priest. Do you remember the story of the Trojan War? The Trojan prince Paris declared Venus to be the most beautiful of all goddesses and therefore she allowed him to marry the most beautiful girl in the world. Unfortunately this was Helen, the wife of Menelaus, king of Sparta. Paris kidnapped her and took her to Troy and so the Greek started a war. This war lasted for ten years and was only decided by a trick by Odysseus, a famous Greek hero.

One morning the Greek left the beach where they were based and just left an enormous wooden horse in front of the gate of Troy. Of course the Trojans did not know what to do with this horse. What would you do if you woke up one morning and a wooden horse was standing in your doorstep? So they debated and one priest did not like the horse. He had a premonition. He warned the Trojans not to take in the horse. But then two snakes came from the sea and devoured him and his sons. The Trojans thought this meant the gods wanted them to take in the horse. So they did and in the night the Greek warriors came out of the belly of the horse, opened the city gate and Troy was destroyed.

It is an amazing statue. You can see the fear and pain in the expressions. Even in antiquity this was a very famous piece. It was lost for many years but then it was found again in 1506 on Esquiline hill. Pope Julius II bought it immediately and brought it here. The right arm of the statue was missing so Michelangelo made a new one. Then centuries later, in 1905, the original arm was found in an antique shop. You can still see Michelangelo's arm in the photo in front of the statue.

After this statue was found, it had an enormous influence on later artists. You can notice, looking at other statues in this courtyard, that there is a lot more emotion and movement in this statue. So centuries after it was made it was a major influence on the development of baroque sculpture.

5.12 Mosaics

When you enter the next room look down. These are mosaics from the second century AD. These mosaics were brought in piece by piece from one of the ancient baths in Rome. You see this a lot in these museums and in palaces from this time. If some beautiful ancient mosaics were discovered, they were taken out and put in the palace of a nobleman or cardinal. Often, if a part was missing, it was restored. Further ahead in the museum you will see more, even more impressive mosaics.

5.13 Room of the Animals

On your right you will see the Room of the Animals. Sometimes, this room is closed and you can only see it from behind a cord. If it's open, just stroll through it. You can see many beautiful statues of animals. They are all ancient, but often heavily restored in the 19th century. Romans really liked these kinds of statues. They really liked representations of day to day life in their homes.

5.14 Mithras

The room to the left is often closed. You can still see it from behind the cord. If you can walk in the most interesting statues are the Marine Centaur with Nereid's and cupids dates back to the first century before Christ. You might also be able to see the statue of

Meleager, the boar hunter. This one is from the first century AD. There is also a nice Mithras group. The cult of Mithras came from Persia and became very popular in Rome at the same time of Christianity. The cult believed that the shedding of the bull's blood marked the beginning of the creation. You can see the little three-headed devil by his knee that tries to stop Mithras from killing the bull.

5.15 The room of the muses

Image 19 CC BY-SA 3.0 Wikimedia Commons

The next room is the Room of the Muses. You can see the muses standing with their backs to the wall all around the room. They are meant to be seen only from the front. The room was designed by Michelangelo Simonetti (a different Michelangelo) and the ceilings were frescoed by Tommaso Conca at the end of the 18th century. The muses are seven daughters of Jupiter and they represent different arts, like song and poetry. They were found in 1774 near Tivoli, a small town near Rome.

The statue in the middle is very important and is called the Belvedere Torso. We do not know who it represents, but this torso was of an immense influence on the art of Michelangelo. You can clearly see how. Look at the muscles and the pose. There is a lot of tension in the body. This is a technique Michelangelo would use extensively to make statues livelier. Remember the static Roman statues you have seen before? This is something else. It is an original Greek statue as you can see by the inscription in the front. It is signed with the name Apollonius. This piece was found in the 15th century at the site of the Roman baths of Caracalla near the Circus Maximus. It is believed to be Hercules, because of the lion skin he is sitting on.

Now try to remember this statue, because you will be able to see it about twenty times in Michelangelo's fresco of the Sistine Chapel. There you will see a lot of naked figures, called Ignudi. He used these figures as some sort of decoration. You will be able to see that Michelangelo painted the torso belvedere from different positions with different heads and feet and managed to create twenty different naked figures like this. He also used it for the body of Christ in his fresco of the last judgment.

5.16 The round room

Image 20 CC BY-SA 3.0 Wikimedia Commons

This room is the Round Room. This room was also designed by Michelangelo Simonetti. Does it remind you of something? Well it should. It is clearly based on the Pantheon. If you have not seen the Pantheon yet, please go. It is amazing.

The mosaic floors in this room date back to the second century BC and depicts the battle of the Centaurs. This mosaic came from bathhouses in Ostia, the old port of Rome. These mosaics were brought here and put on the floor piece by piece.

5.17 Nero's bathtub

In the center of the Round Room stands a monolithic basin. It is made out of one piece of porphyry. It comes from the time of Emperor Nero. He is one of the most infamous emperors. According to legend he was responsible for the famous fire in Rome in 64 AD. It is said that Nero fiddled while Rome burnt. He used the empty space the fire created to build his enormous golden house. This bath stood in that house. He famously said when he moved in; 'Finally I can live like a human being'. The bath is made of red porphyry. This material was known as the Emperor's marble, because purple was the color of the Emperors and the material at that time could only be found in a remote place in Egypt. It still is extremely expensive material.

As so many Emperors, Nero did not die of natural causes. He committed suicide after his armies rose up against him. His famous last words were: 'Qualis artifex pereo': What an artist dies in me. His house was afterwards torn down and the Colosseum was built on top of parts of it.

5.18 Antinous

The statue on the right next to the door you came through is a statue of Antinous. In this room you can also see a bust of the same boy. Look if you can discover him. It should not be too difficult, the faces of the two statues are exactly the same. Antinous was the lover of an Emperor. This was Emperor Hadrian, famous for building a wall to keep out the Scots in England and for building the Pantheon. Hadrian met him in Greece when Antinous was just a boy and the Emperor was 54. Antinous accompanied Hadrian on his many travels until the boy drowned in Egypt in the Nile. Hadrian was struck with grief and declared the boy a god. He then ordered statues to be made to be worshipped throughout the empire. This is way the face of Antinous is one of the best known faces from antiquity. You can see a bust a Hadrian next to the bronze statue of Hercules. You can always recognize Hadrian because he had a beard. He was the first emperor to have a beard, which he wore according to Greek fashion.

5.19 Hercules

Image 21 by Jastrow Wikimedia Commons

The other very famous statue in this room is the bronze Hercules. It was found in 1864 close to Campo de' Fiori. It is one of the very few original bronze statues left from ancient times. Many were melted down. This one survived and we know why. It was buried because it was struck by lightning. Lightning was the symbol of Jupiter, the most important god. The romans were very superstitious people so when this statue was struck they thought Jupiter does not like this statue. So they buried it deep in the ground. So thanks to Jupiter we still have this amazing bronze statue.

5.20 Emperor Galba

There is also a big statue of a man sitting. This is a statue of Emperor Galba. He is not a very famous Emperor, because he was only Emperor for seven months. In the civil war following Nero's death Galba promised the Praetorian Guard (the Emperor's personal army) riches if they supported him to become emperor.

Once Galba was emperor he refused to pay up and the Praetorian Guard then murdered him.

5.21 Emperor Claudius

The next statue is of Emperor Claudius. Claudius was one of the few family members of notorious Emperor Caligula that was not killed by him, because Caligula thought his uncle Claudius was retarded. Claudius lisped and often had drool coming from his mouth and probably had epileptic attacks. That is why his whole family thought he was harmless. When Caligula was murdered, the Praetorian Guard proclaimed Claudius Emperor, because he promised them money and he was the only one of the imperial family still alive. Claudius turned out to be a decent emperor and was not retarded at all. It was under Claudius that Britain was conquered. You can clearly see that the Emperors were displayed as gods. It is very unlikely Claudius had a body like that of his statue.

5.22 The room of the Greek cross

The next room is called the Room of the Greek Cross. It was also designed by Michelangelo Simonetti, in 1780. If you look behind you next to the door you can see two Egyptian statues. They are not real Egyptian, but roman fake Egyptian. They were made for Emperor Hadrian's villa in Tivoli and that is where they were found.

5.23 Porphyry tombs

Image 22 CC BY-SA 2.0 Wikimedia Commons

The two sarcophagi are from the fourth century AD and are made are porphyry, the same material as Nero's bathtub in the last room. Look at them. One was meant for Emperor Constantine's father and one was meant for his daughter. Which one is which do you think? Clearly the one with the angel-like figures and vines was made for his daughter and the one with the warriors on horseback was made for his father. Constantine was a very important Emperor, maybe the most influential of them all, because it was Constantine who made the empire Christian and it was Constantine who built the first Saint Peter's Basilica. Later we will talk some more about him.

5.24 Mosaic of Pallas Athena

The mosaic in the middle represents the goddess Pallas Athena and is from the third century AD. She is the goddess of wisdom, courage and justice.

5.25 The sphinxes

The two sphinxes came from Hadrian's villa and are not Egyptian but Roman.

5.26 Emperor Hadrian

Next to the stairs on the wall you can see another bust of Hadrian. Do you recognize him yet? He is the one with the beard. Hadrian started a new fashion. Before him, romans were clean shaven. Hadrian loved Greek culture and the Greek often had beards. Hadrian broke with the tradition of shaving and many people followed him. Even Emperors that succeeded him were wearing beards.

5.27 The Egyptian museum

To the left is the Egyptian museum. Pope Gregory XVI founded the Gregorian Egyptian Museum in 1839. Here you can find monuments and artefacts of ancient Egypt that came from Rome and from Villa Adriana. Other artifacts came from private collections. The Popes' interest in Egypt came from the role Egypt played in the Sacred Scripture in the History of Salvation.

The Egyptian Museum occupies nine rooms divided by a large hemicycle that opens towards the Cortile della Pigna. You can find many sculptures in these rooms. The last two rooms have artifacts from ancient Mesopotamia, from Syria and Palestine.

6. THE VATICAN MUSEUMS 3: GALLERIA DELLA CANDELABRA

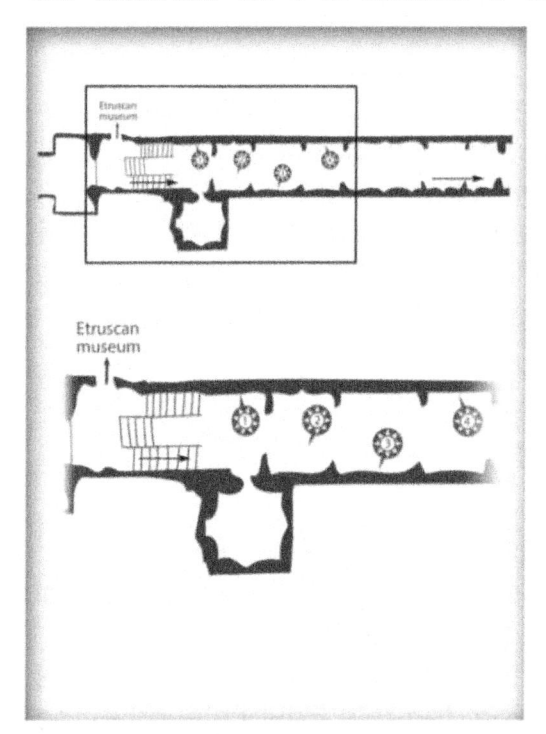

6.1 The view

When you move out of the Room of the Greek Cross and up the stairs, you can have a look out the window with a nice view back to the Cortile della Pigna. In this room many Popes would stay during the summer, because it is one of the few places in the Vatican where you can enjoy a nice breeze. The Vatican is very hot in the summer. That is why nowadays the Pope stays outside Rome in the summer in Castel Gandolfo.

The small room on the other side of the window houses a few very beautiful roman statues. Statues and sarcophagi depict scenes from athletic competitions and circus games. You can see athletes throwing discus, wrestling, and competing in chariot races. The antique works are positioned around a beautiful marble chariot which stands in the middle.

This amazing sculpture is made up of both ancient parts and restoration work by Francesco Antonio Franzoni. In 1788, the sculptor brought together the ancient pieces of the chariot and one of the horses. He then carved a second horse. The newer horse is the one on the left.

6.2 Galleria della Candelabra

The next room is the Galleria della Candelabra, named after the candle holders in the niches. This used to be open loggia. There was no roof here, but Michelangelo Simonetti closed it in the 18th century. Notice how the floor goes downhill. When this was still an open space, the slanting floor would help rain water flow away.

Have a look at the beautiful marble floors. The ceilings were painted very late for the Vatican. They are from 1883 and were painted by Domenico Torti and Ludwig Seitz under Pope Leo XIII.

This room is filled with statues but most of them are not very famous or important. They were all found buried around Rome and many have an alcoholic theme. You will see many people drinking or drunk and have something to do with the cult of Bacchus (Latin) or Dionysus (Greek), the god of wine, madness and ecstasy.

6.2 Diana

On your right you will see a goddess with what looks like a lot of breasts. She is Diana, or Artemis in Greek. She is the goddess of hunting and fertility. For a long time people thought she had a lot of breasts but often she is also depicted as a normal human looking god. Look to the statue facing Diana on the other side of the hall. This also is Diana but represented in a more normal fashion. We know Diana had an important cult in Ephese in Greece. The problem is the cult was secret so nothing about it ever was written down. We know it was very important but we know little about it. Nowadays some archaeologists think that they are not breasts but represent the testicles of bulls which were a symbol of male fertility.

6.3 Bacchus

The next statue that is of interest is the one on the left side of the hall. It is Bacchus, the God of Wine. He is carrying a little boy on his back. It is very famous because it still has the original glass eyes. Before, many statues had glass eyes. Unfortunately many of these eyes were broken when the barbarians invaded Italy. They thought the eyes were made out of precious stones, but they were just made out of glass.

Maybe you notice that a lot of statues are dressed in a fig leaf. This is absolutely not classical. The Romans never had any problems with nudity, or sexuality for that matter. Most private parts of the statues were taken off in the 17th and 18th century and replaced with fig leaves, because the Popes thought the statues to be too indecent to show naked.

7. THE VATICAN MUSEUMS 4: GALLERY OF THE TAPESTRIES

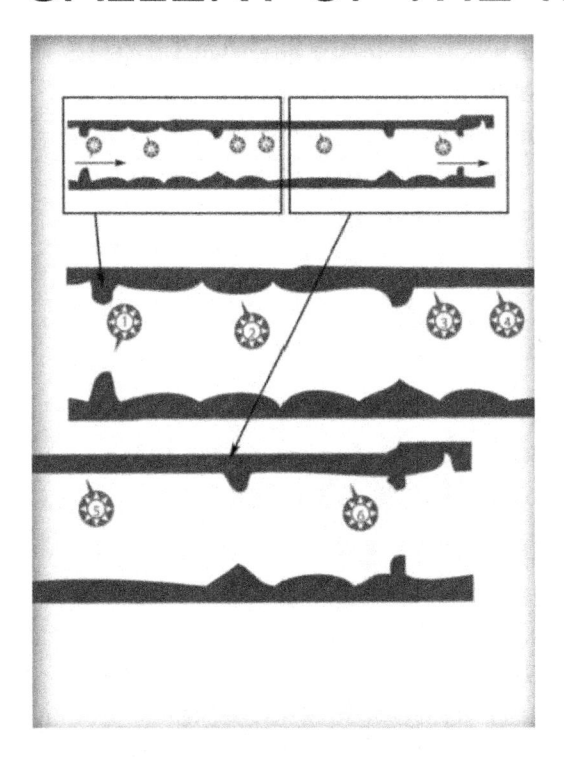

7.1 Galleria delle Arreze

The next room is the Gallery of the Tapestries. On the left wall you can see tapestries representing the life of Christ. They are based on designs by the school of Raphael, but they were woven in Flanders, where the best weavers could be found. They were commissioned by Clement VII in the 1500s. The ones on the right tell the life of Urban VIII. He was a pope from the Barberini family. I have talked a bit about this Pope when I talked about the Baldacchino by Bernini in Saint Peter's. Urban VIII was one of Bernini's most important patrons.

These tapestries about the life of Urban VIII were woven here in Rome and you can see the difference in quality. Clearly the Flemish weavers were a lot better at weaving.

It would take nine years to finish just one Flemish tapestry. They are made out of the most precious materials like gold thread, silk, silver thread and wool. They were not only made to decorate walls but also to keep out the heat or the cold in summer or winter. They would give extra isolation. I will concentrate on the tapestries on the left because they are the most interesting.

7.2 *The ceiling and the first tapestries*

The first tapestry on the left shows the birth of Jesus. The next one is more interesting because it shows baby Jesus being circumcised by a Pope. Of course no popes existed back then.

While you pass the tapestries do not forget to look up. The ceilings look like they are carved, but they are not. They are painted. It is a technique called *Chiaroscuro*. The artist paints shadows to make his painting look three-dimensional. They were painted in 1789 by Domenico Del Frate and Antonio Marini and depict allegorical scenes celebrating the glory of the reigning Pope, Pius VI.

7.3 *Transfiguration*

The next tapestry shows the Transfiguration. Jesus shows his true godly nature to three apostles. He begins to shine with white bright light and then Moses and Elijah appear next to him. Then a voice from the sky calls him son. Did you go to the Pinacoteca to see Raphael's painting of the Transfiguration? That painting is more impressive than this tapestry.

7.4 Massacre of the innocents

The next three tapestries depict the massacre of the innocents and on the first you can see the Pantheon on the top left. Herod ordered the execution of all young male children in the vicinity of Bethlehem, to avoid be dethroned by a newborn King of the Jews whose birth had been announced to him by the Magi. It is not a very pleasant scene to look at, but it is a very common theme in religious art from the middle ages and renaissance.

7.5 Resurrection

The next tapestry represents the resurrection of Christ. After the Romans crucified Jesus, he was anointed and buried in a new tomb by Joseph of Arimathea. God raised him from the dead after three days and he appeared to many people over a span of forty days before he ascended into heaven. This is the most famous tapestry. As you walk past it you have to keep on looking into the eyes of Christ. You will see that he looks at you from every angle. This is of course symbolic. Christ watches over you. The effect is really well done. The technique was used in painting more often, like in Leonardo da Vinci's Mona Lisa, but to create the same effect in tapestry is very difficult. It involves a complex system of cross-stitching.

7.6 Murder of Caesar

The last two tapestries on your left before you enter the next Gallery are different. They do not depict the life of Christ, but scenes from Roman times. The last one is the most interesting. Here we see the murder of Julius Caesar by 60 senators. This happened on the Ides of March in 44 BC, which is the 15th of March. The senators were afraid that Caesar wanted to become king. At that time Rome was a republic, but Caesar had been ruling as a Dictator for many years. The senators wanted Rome to stay a republic, but unfortunately for them after the murder, Caesar's adopted son Octavian won a civil war and became the first Imperator, or Emperor and took the name Augustus. This was the end of the republic system and the start of the Roman Empire.

8. THE VATICAN MUSEUMS 5: GALLERY OF THE MAPS

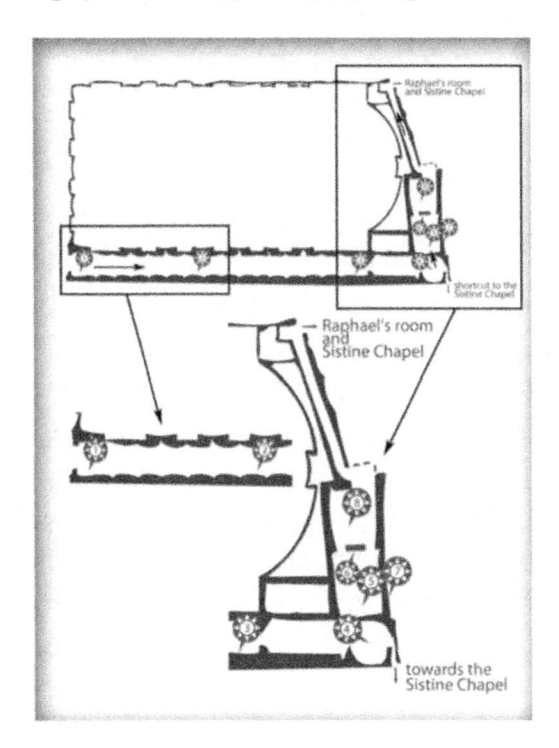

8.1 The Gallery of the maps

Image 23 by Jean-Pol GRANDMONT Wikimedia Commons

    The next gallery is called the Gallery of the Maps. It was commissioned by Pope Gregory XIII in 1582. It is 120 meters long. It was painted and designed by the most famous cartographers of the time, who were led by Ignazio Danti, a Dominican monk. They went out and studied all of Italy and then produced these maps. They are very accurate. If you compare them with modern maps they are about 84% accurate. This is an amazing achievement because they did not have modern technology like aerial photography and satellites.

    There are 40 maps in this room. You have to imagine you are walking on the Apennine Mountains, so all the maps to your left represent the west side of Italy and all the maps on your right represent the east of Italy. But beware; sometimes north and south are reversed.

    Besides Italy you will see immediately on your left a map of the area around Avignon in France, which at that time was part of the Papal possessions. The maps are a valuable source of information, because many of these villages you see on the maps now have disappeared. Many villages only live on in the last name of Italians who often took their last name from the place they were from, unless they were of noble birth. Leonardo is called da Vinci, because he was from Vinci, a small village in Tuscany.

In the maps you can also see some famous historical battles being depicted, like the battle of Trasimeno where Hannibal defeated the Romans.

Image 24 by Jean-Pol GRANDMONT CC BY-SA 3.0 Wikimedia Commons

Do not forget to look at the ceilings. They are breathtaking. We see eighty episodes from the history of the Catholic Church and the lives of the Saints. All the stories that are painted took place in the territory beneath it. They were painted in the 1600s by many different artists. The two lead painters were Girolamo Muziano and Cesare Nebbia.

In 1631 Pope Urban VIII had the maps completed and embellished with additional ornamental elements by Lucas Holste.

8.2 Vatican City State

As you walk through the gallery do not forget to look to your right out the window. You will have a lovely view into the Vatican gardens. On the hill you can see a big radio tower which is used to broadcast the radio channel of the Vatican.

The total territory of the Vatican is 110 acres, which is 44 hectares. Within the walls only 900 people live, 700 men and 200 women. The Vatican is a country. The Pope is the head of state. The Vatican is the only absolute monarchy left in Europe. The Vatican issues its own passports and license plates, but very few people have Vatican nationality. Often people obtain Vatican nationality for the duration of their assignment. The Vatican has their own euros but they are difficult to obtain. You can buy them for a lot of money in collectors' stores. The Vatican also has a TV network and a radio station. Inside the Vatican, there are government offices and courthouses, grocery stores and pharmacies. The Vatican has a fire department and its own military corps, the Swiss Guards. There are about a hundred guards now, but before it was a real army. The corps was founded by Pope Julius II, who just wanted Swiss mercenaries, because at that time the Swiss were the best and most organized fighters of Europe.

To be a Swiss Guard you have to be between 19 and 25 years old. You have to be Swiss. They often come from the Italian speaking part of Switzerland. You cannot have a police record, not even a parking ticket. You have to come from a good catholic home and you are not allowed to marry while you serve the Pope. They are trained in about 600 different weapons so they can pick up anything on the floor and kill you with it.

They live within the walls and do not pay rent or food. It is considered an honorary job. Afterwards it is very easy for them to find a job in Switzerland, because the job is still very high regarded.

8.3 Last maps

Before you go to the next room have a look at the maps at the end of the gallery. On your right there is a map of Italia Antica. This shows how Italy used to be in Roman times. Then on your left there is a map of Italia Nova. This shows Italy how it was at the time the maps were commissioned.

Next to the door you can see four frescos of the most important ports at the time: Venice, Genua, Cività Vecchia and Ancona.

8.4 Crossroads

In this room you have to make a choice. You can decide to go straight ahead and go directly to the Sistine Chapel or you can go left and visit Raphael's rooms and then go through the museum of modern art and then go to the Sistine Chapel. From the Sistine Chapel you cannot go back and see Raphael's rooms.

8.5 Sobieski room

This room is called the king Sobieski Room and is named after the huge painting by the Polish artist Jan Matejko. It shows the victory of the king of Poland John III Sobieski, who stopped the Ottoman Turks from invading Vienna in 1683. Thanks to Sobieski Europe was not overrun by the Turks. The painting was donated to the Pope by the Artist in the 1800s. All the other paintings in here also date back to 1800s.

8.6 The martyrs of Gorkum

Next to the door is a painting of the Martyrs of Gorkum. These 19 catholic Dutch Franciscans were hanged by the Protestants on 9 July 1572 in the Dutch religious wars. They were canonized on 29 June 1865 by the pope in Rome. The painting is by Cesare Fracassini.

8.7 View of the Sistine chapel

If you look out of the window you can see a building on the other side. This is the Sistine Chapel from the outside. As you can see it was built as a fort. Look at the top of the building where you can see places where archers could shoot from.

8.8 The room of the Immaculate Conception

This room is called the Room of Immaculate Conception. This room is situated on what was once the Borgia Tower. The Frescos here were painted by Francesco Podesti in the 19th century. They show scenes from the proclamation of the Dogma of the Immaculate Conception by Pope Pius IX in 1854.

The doctrine refers to the conception of the Virgin Mary in the womb of her mother Anne. According to the doctrine Anne's womb was without sin and so the Virgin Mary was born free of original sin and therefore Christ was born free of sin. The document was proclaimed Ex Cathedra. When a dogma is proclaimed Ex Cathedra it can no longer be changed. This was the last time a dogma was proclaimed in this way. The papal bull was sent to every country in the world and as was the custom the countries sent it back to the Vatican translated into their own language. These documents are kept in this beautiful cabinet which was made in Paris.

9. THE VATICAN MUSEUM 6: RAPHAEL'S ROOMS

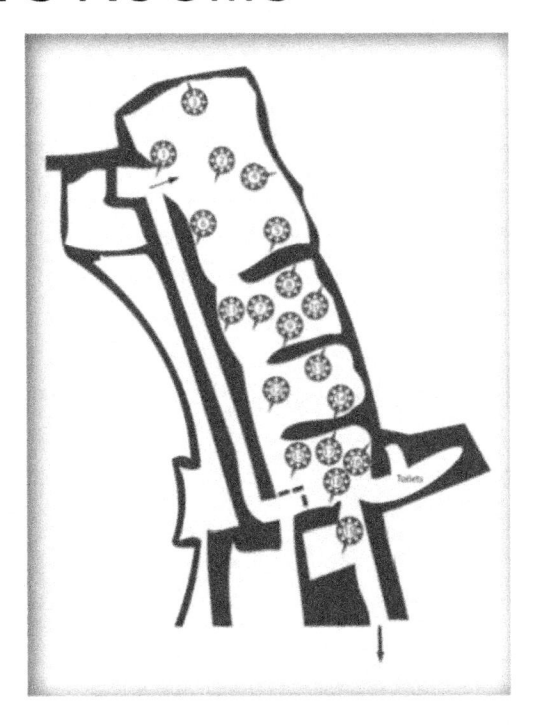

9.1 Rooms of Rafael

You will now enter the Raphael rooms. They would have been Julius II private apartments. He moved here because he did not want to live in the apartments of one of his predecessors and his archenemy, Rodrigo Borgia, Pope Alexander VI. Also, he thought the ceilings of the Borgia apartments were painted with scenes of debauchery. Donato Bramante, the famous first architect of the new Saint Peters, suggested Raphael Sanzio to Julius II for the painting of the rooms. Raphael was only 25 at the time and not a very well-known artist. It took a total of 16 years to complete all the rooms.

Raphael worked on them from 1508 to 1520, but then he died, so the rooms were finished by his students.

9.2 The room of Constantine

The first room is the room of Constantine. It is the first room we enter, but it was the last to be painted. This room was used for receptions and official ceremonies. It's based on designs by Raphael, but all done by his students, like Giulio Romano. His students started painting in 1517 and finished in 1524. The main theme of the room is the Triumph of Christianity over Paganism. If you look up to the ceiling you can see this theme depicted. A roman statue of a god lies broken on the floor while a crucifix is standing up.

The four major paintings show scenes from the life of Emperor Constantine, the important emperor who legalized Christianity.

9.3 The vision of Constantine

In the first fresco you can see the Vision of the Cross. Constantine wanted to become to sole ruler of the Roman Empire and so he had to defeat his rival Maxentius. Before the final battle he had a vision. An angel appeared and told him that if he fought in the sign of the cross he would be victories. The angel said 'In hoc signo Vinces', in this sign you will conquer. You can see the words the angel is saying (in Greek) in the fresco. It meant that Constantine would be victorious if he substituted the imperial eagles on the soldiers' standards with the cross. The next day Constantine had crosses painted on all of his soldier's shields and in the battle at the Milvian Bridge he was victorious. You can see Constantine in his camp standing in front of his tent looking up to the sign of the cross in the sky.

Also note the view of Rome with many recognizable monuments in the background.

9.4 The battle at the Milvian Bridge

The next fresco depicts the Battle at the Milvian Bridge. This is a bridge north of Rome which still exists. You can see Constantine victorious. He is the one on the white horse with a golden armor and a spear in his hands. The evil Maxentius drowns in the Tiber on his brown horse, looking at Constantine. You can also see that Constantine is protected by Saint Peter and Saint Paul. They fly above Constantine during the battle. This battle represents the victory of Christianity over Paganism.

In the background you can see Monte Mario, where the Villa Madama can be seen, a villa that Raphael had designed for the Pope. Raphael most certainly planned these frescos, but it was his famous student Giulio Romano who painted it, after the death of the master.

9.5 The baptism of Constantine

In the next fresco you can see the Baptism of Constantine. According to legend, Constantine suffered of leprosy and his pagan advisers advised him to bathe in an innocent's child blood. St Peter and St Paul appeared to him and told him to find Pope Sylvester I. Constantine then was baptized by the pope and miraculously cured.

This legend seems to be a fabrication however. Most historians agree that if Constantine ever was baptized it was just before dying, because he believed it was impossible to be a good emperor and a good Christian at the same time.

What is certain is that Constantine legalized Christianity in the year 313 with the edict of Milan. The influence of Constantine on western history was almost unparalleled because of this. Before the emperor started to favor Christianity about 5% of the population of the empire was Christian. After Constantine about 60% became Christian.

The Pope in the fresco has the traits of Clement VII. During his pontificate the work on this fresco was resumed. The fresco is attributed to Giovan Francesco Penni.

9.6 The donation of Constantine

The last fresco is the Donation of Constantine. For a long time it was believed that when Constantine left Rome to found Constantinople, he left his temporal power to Pope Sylvester I. The church was in possession of a document that claimed the papacy was the rightful ruler of the whole western world. For a long time popes based their temporal power on this document.

In the renaissance this document was discovered to be a forgery. Lorenzo Valla who was an Italian Catholic priest and Renaissance humanist was one of the first who exposed this forgery in 1440. The Latin used could never have been written in the time of Constantine and it was clear the document was written many centuries after the death of Constantine. On the fresco we see the emperor kneeling before the Pope. This is pure propaganda! It seems the church is saying that Emperors should kneel for Popes.

The Pope in the fresco again has the traits of Clement VII and the episode takes place in the interior of the old basilica of St Peter's, which was later destroyed. It was most likely painted by Gianfrancesco Penni or Giulio Romano, somewhere between 1520 and 1524.

9.7 The room of Heliodorus

The next room is the Room of Heliodorus, painted from 1512-1514. This room was originally used for the private audiences of the Pope and was decorated by Raphael immediately after the Stanza della Segnatura, making it the second room to be painted. The theme of the frescos in this room is political. The frescos document the protection that God has bestowed on the church, throughout history. In this time Pope Julius II was trying to free Italy from the French, who, under King Charles VIII, had occupied most of the peninsula. The frescos are showing how God always protects the faith and the church. They can be seen as some sort of warning to the French.

9.8 The expulsion of Heliodorus

The first fresco depicts the Expulsion of Heliodorus from the Temple. This fresco was completed by Raphael himself. It shows the biblical story of Heliodorus from 2 Maccabees, 3:21-28, who was sent by the king of Syria Seleucus, to take over the treasure preserved in the temple of Jerusalem.

In the fresco, you see Heliodorus lying on the ground on the right. Onias, the high priest on the left prayed to God for assistance. God then sent a horseman, assisted by two youths, to beat and banish Heliodorus. The High Priest is a portrait of Pope Julius II. Raphael has also added a portrait of himself next to the people carrying away the Pope.

9.9 Attila

The next fresco shows the meeting of Pope Leo I with Attila the Hun. It was completed after the death of Julius II, during the pontificate of his successor Leo X (pontiff from 1513 to 1521).

Attila the Hun is convinced by Pope Leo the Great not to attack Rome in 452. This really happened. We don't know exactly how Leo did it, but the fact is Attila retreated after meeting the pope outside the city gates. Here we see Leo is assisted by Saint Peter and Saint Paul, who frighten Attila in retreating.

If you look at the face of the cardinal in the forefront behind the Pope and then look at the face of the Pope. You can see that it is the same face. Julius II died and the cardinal depicted was elected the new Pope. He took the name of Leo X, the same name as the Pope in the story, Leo I. Raphael changed the face of Leo I in the fresco to the face of the new Pope, Leo X.

Raphael places the scene at the gates of Rome. You can see the Colosseum, an aqueduct, an obelisk and other buildings in the background. However, the historical event took place in the north of Italy, near Mantua.

9.10 The mass at Bolsena

This fresco shows the miraculous event of the Mass at Bolsena. It depicts an episode that took place in 1263 in Bolsena, near Orvieto. A Bohemian priest had doubts about the transubstantiation. This means he did not believe in the changing of the substance of the bread and wine into that of the body and blood of Christ in the Eucharist. During a mass he saw blood pour out of the sacred host and his doubts disappeared.

The miracle led to the establishment of the feast of Corpus Christi and the construction of the cathedral of Orvieto, a beautiful cathedral, well worth a visit.

You can see Pope Julius II, always recognizable by his long white beard, kneeling in front of the priest. You can also see the Swiss guards down below.

9.11 The liberation of Peter

One of Raphael's masterpieces is the liberation of St. Peter above the window. Here we see the story of how an angel appeared to St Peter who was locked up in prison. The angel asked him to stand up and when he did his chains fell off and the angel led him out into the street, while the guards were sleeping (Acts of the Apostles 12:5-12).

You can see the guards waking up in bewilderment to find out that the prisoner is missing. If you look at the face of Saint Peter you can see that it is the face of Julius II. This fresco is considered a masterpiece because of the light that emanates from it and the nice contrast which is created by the darkness of the prison bars. The bars were not painted *al secco*, or added on later. They were incorporated into the fresco at same time. This is very difficult to do.

This scene is a reference to Pope Julius II, who before becoming Pope was the titular cardinal of St. Peter in Chains, a church in Rome where Saint Peter's chains are held.

9.12 Stanza della segnatura

The Room of the Segnatura, which was painted from 1508 to 1511, contains Raphael's most famous frescos. The room was used by Julius II as his library and private office, but afterwards it became the room where most important Papal documents were signed and sealed. So it is called the room of the *segnatura*, which means signing. The room contains the first work of Raphael in the Vatican.

The frescos depict the three greatest categories of the human spirit: Truth, Good and Beauty. Godly Truth is illustrated in the Disputation of the Most Holy Sacrament, which alludes to the science of theology, while rational Truth is depicted in the School of Athens. In this famous fresco you can see the science of philosophy. Good is expressed in the Cardinal and Theological Virtues and the Law. Beauty is shown in the Parnassus with Apollo and the Muses.

9.13 The school of Athens

The School of Athens is the most important fresco in this room. This fresco depicts rational wisdom. We see a debate on the search for truth between the Greek philosophers Plato and Aristotle. They are the two figures in the middle both holding their most famous books in their hand. Plato holds his book the Timaeus and Aristotle his Ethica. Raphael gave Plato the face of Leonardo da Vinci, putting him at par with Plato. Aristotle is on his right. Many figures have the faces of Raphael's contemporaries, but unfortunately we are not quite sure who is who. Some figures however are recognizable.

On the right we see Euclid, who is teaching geometry to his pupils. He is shown as a bent over bald man explaining a theory with a compass and he has the face of Raphael's friend Donato Bramante, the first architect to work on the new Saint Peters for Pope Julius II. The architectural space in which the figures stand is clearly inspired by Bramante's work.

Raphael worked in this room at the same time Michelangelo was painting the ceiling of the Sistine Chapel. According to legend Raphael sometimes would sneak in in to see what Michelangelo was doing and was really inspired by what he saw. You can clearly see the influence of Michelangelo in the big and strong figures in this fresco.

Raphael also painted Michelangelo in his fresco. He is depicted as the pessimist philosopher, Heracleitus. He is leaning against a block of marble on the steps, writing on a sheet of paper. Michelangelo was an artist who was always by himself and a bit of a loner so that's why he is sitting by himself on the steps.

Raphael also added a self-portrait. You can see him to the far right behind the person in white (this is a portrait of Sodoma, who was Raphael's teacher). Raphael is the one with the black hat.

9.14 The disputation of the holy sacrament

On the other side of the wall you can see the disputation of the holy sacrament. This fresco shows the other form of wisdom, which is theological wisdom. So together with the school of Athens all forms of wisdom are represented: Godly and humanly wisdom. We see Popes and Saints on earth debating about the nature of the holy sacrament and above, up in heaven the same debate is being held. On the vertical axis you can see the holy trinity. High above in the middle you see God, right under him Jesus and under Jesus you can see a dove representing the Holy Spirit.

Christ sits between the Virgin and St John the Baptist. Around them, seated on the clouds of heaven, you can see patriarchs and prophets of the Old Testament alternated with apostles and martyrs. The personages are (from left to right) St. Peter, Adam, St. John the Evangelist, David, St. Laurence, Judas Maccabees, St. Stephen, Moses, St. James the elder, Abraham and St. Paul.

On the ground, close to the altar sit the four Fathers of the Latin Church. They are St. Gregory the Great (a portrait of Julius II), St. Jerome, St. Ambrose and St. Augustine. In the other figures on the ground you can see the portrait of Sixtus IV (Julius II's uncle) in the pontiff furthest to the right, Dante Alighieri behind him and Beato Angelico, the painter, as the monk on the extreme left.

9.15 Stanza del incendio

This room is called the Room of the Fire in the Borgo. *Incendio* means fire in Italian. The room was used in the time of Julius for the meetings of the highest court of the Holy See. At the time of Leo X the room was used as a dining room. This Pope gave Raphael the commission to fresco the walls. Raphael then entrusted a large part of the work to his pupils. The work was completed between 1514 and 1517. The scenes in the frescos depict the lives of previous Popes that were also called Leo.

9.16 The fire in the borgo

The most famous fresco in this room was done by Raphael himself and it is called the Fire in the Borgo. It celebrates a miracle that took place in 847. There was a great fire in the Borgo, which is the residential area around the Vatican. Pope Leo IV appeared on the balcony and made the sign of the cross and the fire was miraculously extinguished. The fresco is interesting because behind the Pope we can see the façade of the old Saint Peter's, the basilica that was built in the time of Emperor Constantine.

The figures on the left on the forefront are an allusion to the story of Aeneas who is fleeing from a burning Troy. He is considered the forefather of the roman people. You see him escaping with his son and with his father on his back. The Vestal Virgin Rhea Silvia, who was the mother of the twins Romulus and Remus was a direct descendant of Aeneas and it was Romulus who founded Rome, the city that still bears his name.

9.17 The battle of Ostia

The rest of the room was done by students. In this fresco you can see the Battle of Ostia. Here we see Leo IV (pontiff from 847 to 855) and his troops winning a battle against the Saracens at Ostia, then the harbor of Rome. The fresco refers to the crusade against the infidels that Pope Leo X (the Pope who commissioned the work) wanted.

9.18 The coronation of Charlemagne

In this fresco you can see the coronation of Charlemagne by Pope Leo III in the year 800. This really happened on Christmas Eve in the old Saint Peter's Basilica. Charlemagne was crowned Emperor by the Pope. This was very important for the papacy, because this way the Pope could say that his authority was higher than that of Emperors. The fresco also refers to the concordat drawn up between the Holy See and the kingdom of France in 1515. Leo III (pontiff from 795 to 816) is depicted as Leo X and Charlemagne is a portrait of Francis I, King of France at the time.

9.19 To the Sistine chapel

This is the end of the Rooms of Raphael. In the Room of the Fire in the Borgo there are some toilets. After, you continue towards the Sistine Chapel. You will pass the Borgia apartments, the museum of modern art and then you will enter the Sistine Chapel.

10. THE VATICAN MUSEUM 7: TOWARDS THE SISTINE CHAPEL

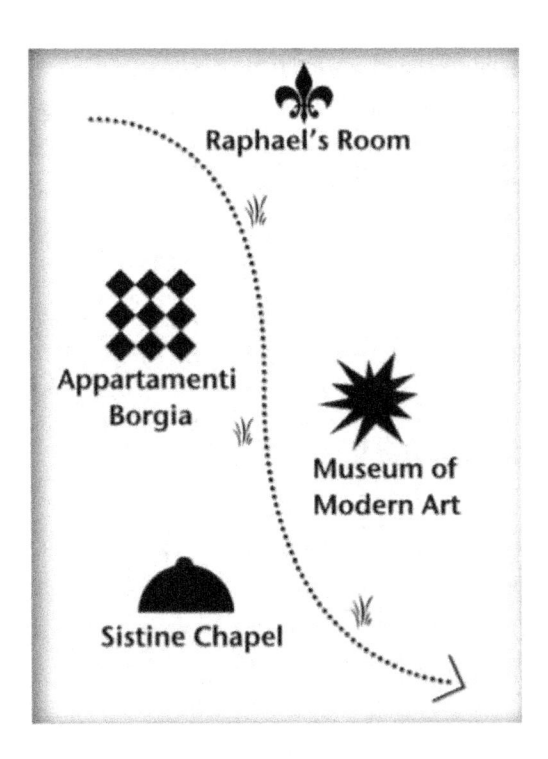

10.1 The Borgia apartments

There is not so much to see in the Borgia Apartments. They are located under the Rooms of Raphael. Pope Julius II did not want to live in these apartments, because Rodrigo Borgia was his archenemy.

The ceilings of these apartments were frescoed by Pinturicchio, a decent painter from Umbria. In the fourth room there is a depiction of the Holy Virgin, which according to legend is a portrait of the lover of the Pope, Giulia Farnese. In the same room there is also a depiction of the condemnation of Saint Catherine of Alexandria. Saint Catherine is a portrait of the daughter of the Pope, Lucrezia Borgia. The figure of the emperor looks a lot like Cesare Borgia, the son of the pope. In the fifth room there is a picture of Alexander himself, kneeling and praying.

Rodrigo Borgia was a Spanish Pope, and a very notorious one. He became pope in 1492. He had many lovers and many children. Lavish, often sexually themed parties were held in the Vatican during his reign. His son Cesare was rumored to have indecent relations with his sister and to have murdered his brother Juan. On him Machiavelli based his famous book The Prince. The Borgias tried to turn Italy into their personal kingdom, but when Alexander died of malaria Cesare had to flee Rome.

10.2 Museum of modern art

In the museum of modern art you can find many artworks by famous modern artists that were gifts to different popes by collectors or artists. Have a look around. There are no very famous paintings here but a lot of famous artists, like Dali, Chagall, Klee, Botero and Francis Bacon.

I especially like the painting by Francis Bacon which was inspired by Velazquez' portrait of Pope Innocent X. It is the painting of a very scary looking pope against a dark background. Bacon was very inspired by Michelangelo in his painting. You can see this in the tension both artists put in their figures. This makes them come alive.

11. THE VATICAN MUSEUMS 8: THE SISTINE CHAPEL CEILING

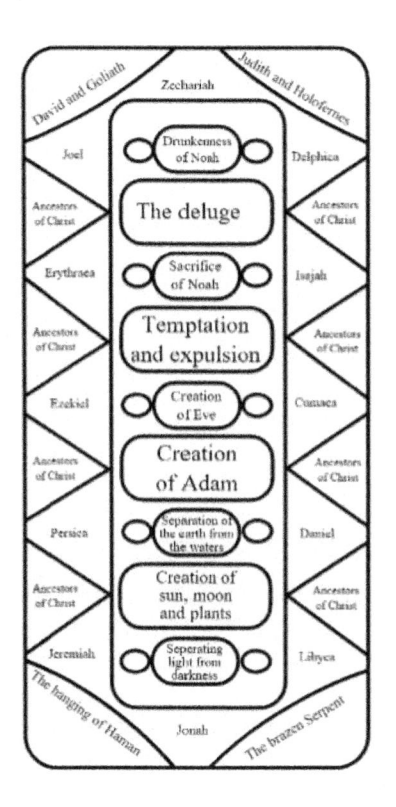

11.1 Sixtus IV

The name Sistine Chapel comes from the Pope who commissioned the Chapel, Pope Sixtus IV of the Della Rovere family. The chapel was designed by Baccio Pontelli and built under the supervision of Giovannino de Dolci between 1473 and 1481. Sixtus built the chapel for different reasons. He wanted a chapel where he could attend mass in private. The Pope did not like to attend mass in Saint Peters, where everybody could see him. Besides that, the Chapel also has a clear defensive function. If you look at it from the outside it looks just like a fort.

It is 22 meters high and also served as a fortress. Its outside is not decorated much, as was the custom in this time. There is no exterior façade. The building consists of three stories. The ground floor has very small windows and an exit to a courtyard. The first floor holds the actual Sistine Chapel. The vault of the chapel rises 20,7 meters high (68ft). Above the vault is another level, with guardrooms.

Another reason to build the chapel was that a place was needed to hold the conclave, the ceremony in which a new Pope is selected. The first mass in the Sistine Chapel was celebrated on 15 August 1483, the Feast of the Assumption, at which ceremony the chapel was consecrated and dedicated to the Virgin Mary.

After the chapel was finished, the ceiling was painted in blue, with gold starts. So the ceiling of the chapel looked nothing like how it looks now, with Michelangelo's beautiful fresco.

Then, Sixtus had the side walls painted by the most famous artists of his time. Painters like Botticelli, famous for painting the birth of Venus, worked in the chapel, but also artists like Perugino from Umbria and Ghirlandaio, who later became Michelangelo's teacher. All these frescoes were considered masterpieces. The artists were just very unlucky that decades later Michelangelo painted one of the most important works in western art on the ceiling of the chapel. So nowadays nobody looks at their frescoes, which is too bad, because they too are masterpieces in their own right.

It is possible that Perugino was supervising the whole project. Some say the fact that Florence's best painters did this work, was because of a reconciliation between Lorenzo de' Medici, the ruler of Florence and Sixtus, who had been at odds. The Florentines started working in 1481.

On one side we have can see scenes from the life of Jesus and the other side scenes from the life of Moses. Above these they painted the first 24 Popes of the Church. The reason that the life of Jesus is painted and the life of Moses on the other side is because the Church wanted to draw a parallel between the Old Testament and the New Testament. It wanted to show the continuity between the two.

Let's look a bit more at these frescos on the side walls. The southern wall is decorated with frescos from the life of Moses. Starting from the altar, you first see Moses leaving to Egypt, by Pietro Perugino.

This fresco shows Moses leaving to Egypt, after he had been exiled from Midian. In all the frescos, Moses is recognizable by his yellow and green robes. Moses is depicted multiple times in this one fresco. This was very common in this time and comes from medieval painting. In the middle you can see an angel asking Moses to circumcise his son as a sign of the alliance between God and the

Israelites. On the right in the fresco you can see the circumcision take place.

The next fresco depicts the trials of Moses and was painted by Sandro Botticelli.

This fresco shows several episodes from when Moses was young, as written in exodus. On the right you can see Moses killing the Egyptian who had harassed a Hebrew, and then fleeing to the desert. In the scene in the middle, you can see Moses fighting the shepherds who refused to let Jethro's daughters let their cattle drink water. After Moses wins, he takes water for them (including his future wife, who is one of the daughters). In the upper left corner, you can see Moses removing his shoes as he receives the task from God to return to Egypt and free his people. In the lower left corner, you can see Moses leading the Jews to the Promised Land.

In detail of the work, you can clearly see that is was Botticelli who painted this work. Botticelli is most famous for the way he depicted women. They often had beautiful faces and blond hair. Maybe you know his painting 'The birth of Venus'. Look at this detail from the fresco in the Sistine Chapel:

The next fresco is called 'The Crossing of the Red Sea'. It is often attributed to Domenico Ghirlandaio, but some art historians don't agree and believe it was painted by Cosimo Rosselli or Biagio d'Antonio.

This scene shows different episodes at the same time, just as the other frescos. In the right background, Moses is asking the Pharaoh to free the Israelites. The most impressive scene is the Egyptian soldiers drowning in the red sea on the right. They are drowning in full battle costume, being led by the Pharaoh, who lets out a big scream before drowning. On the left, Moses is looking at the drowning Egyptians with his Israelites.

The next fresco is by Cosimo Rosselli, who may or may not have also painted the fresco above. This one is called Descent from Mount Sinai.

In the upper part, Moses is kneeling, with a sleeping Joshua. He receives the tables of the law by God, who appears from the cloud on the right. On the left in front you can see Moses bringing the law to the Israelites. In the background you can see them adoring the golden calf, led by Aaron. Right in the middle, we can see an angry Moses breaking the tables of the law in anger on the floor.

Next to this fresco, you can see the Punishment of the Rebels, by Sandro Botticelli.

Again, three episodes are depicted. They all concern a rebellion by the Israelites against Moses and Aaron. The life of the Israelites had become very hard on the road from Egypt. On the right the rebels attempt to stone Moses. Joshua is trying to protect Moses from the stoning, by putting himself between his father and the rebels. In the center scene, the rebels are driven out by Moses and on the right, the main rebels disappear in a hole in the earth.

The last fresco depicts the Testament and Death of Moses. It is painted by Luca Signorelli and Bartolomeo della Gatta. The fresco shows the last episode in Moses' life.

In the background, Moses receives the baton of command by an angel, which gives him the right to finally lead his people to the Promised Land. Up in the middle, Moses descends from a mountain with the baton in his hand. In the foreground, on the right, Moses, who is 120 years old now, is talking to the crowd. He holds the baton. At his feet is the Ark of the Covenant. On the left is the appointment of Joshua as Moses' successor.

On the northern wall, scenes from the life of Jesus are depicted.

The first depicts the Baptism of Christ by Perugino. In the middle, Jesus is baptized by John the Baptist. The landscape includes a symbolic view of Rome, recognizable by a triumphal arch, the Colosseum and the Pantheon. At the sides you can see John the Baptist and Jesus preaching to a crowd. John is standing all the way on the left and Jesus all the way on the right.

The next scene depicts the Temptation of Christ and was painted by Botticelli.

The main episodes in this fresco take place in the upper part. On the left upper part, you can see Jesus, who has been fasting, being tempted by the devil to turn stones into bread. In the middle, Jesus stands on top of the temple in Jerusalem. The devil says Jesus should throw himself down, to test God's promise to protect him. On the right, you can see the devil, who has taken Jesus to a mountain top. He promises Jesus the power over the earth if he bows down to him. Jesus sends the devil away.

In the foreground, you can see a man, who has been healed from leprosy by Jesus, present himself at the temple so he may be proclaimed clean.

In the next fresco, you can see the Vocation of the Apostles.

This was painted by Domenico Ghirlandaio, most famous for being a teacher to Michelangelo and the frescos in the Tornabuoni Chapel in the Santa Maria Novella in Florence. This scene shows fishermen Andrew and Peter, who are on their knees, as they are being called by Jesus.

The next scene depicts the Sermon on the Mount and it is painted by Cosimo Rosselli. After this, you can see the Delivery of the Keys by Perugino.

This scene is a reference to Matthew 16 in which the keys of the kingdom of heaven are given to Saint Peter. This is a very important scene for the Papacy. Jesus hands over his authority to forgive and spread the word of God to Saint Peter. The Popes consider themselves direct successors to Saint Peter, who is considered the first Pope.

The final scene is by Cosimo Rosselli again and represents the Last Supper.

Judas, as usual, is depicted on his side and from behind. Can you see the fighting cat and dog? They are elements which further stress Judas' negative connotation. The scene shows the moment immediately after Jesus' annunciation he will be betrayed by one of the apostles. The apostles are shocked and raise their hands as they discus.

Sixtus IV was a typical Pope of the renaissance. So when he became Pope he made sure he made sure he advanced his family as well as he could. Even nowadays in Italy if you need a job you need to have an uncle somewhere who can help you. This is called nepotism, from the Italian word *nipote*, which means nephew. So when Sixtus became Pope he made sure that all his nephews got good jobs.11.2 Julius II

One of his favorite nephews was Giuliano della Rovere. Immediately when he became Pope Sixtus made him a bishop and cardinal at age 28. At one point he held no less than 28 bishoprics. His ability and personality soon gave him an enormous influence over the College of Cardinals, even after the death of his uncle. Then his archenemy was elected pope. Cardinal Rodrigo Borgia from Spain became Pope Alexander VI. Giuliano accused him of bribing the cardinals to elect him and fled to France, where he convinced King Charles VIII to invade Italy to conquer the kingdom of Naples and depose the Pope. This did not work out as well as Giuliano intended, but after the death of Alexander and a short lived pontificate of Pius III, Giuliano managed to be elected Pope. He did this the same way Rodrigo Borgia had managed to secure the papacy: bribery. Some cardinals were offered money, some nice positions and in 1503 he was elected Pope. He took the name of Julius II.

The names of these renaissance popes already tell you something about them. They are called Alexander, Julius and Leo. These are not very Christian names. Alexander of course refers to Alexander the great, Julius to Caesar.

The papacy of Julius was very important. He was called the warrior pope. He liked to actually lead his troops into battle, something no other pope had done before him. He re-conquered the Papal States and made sure they were firmly under his control. They say he preferred the smell of gunpowder to the smell of incense.

11.3 Patron of the Arts

Besides all these activities on the battlefield Julius was very interested in the arts. He got some of the best artists and architects to Rome to work for him. He got the young Michelangelo to work for him on a tomb. This tomb was to be enormous and was meant to be put in in Saint Peters.

But then the Pope got a better idea. He decided, in order to be really remembered well, he had to start rebuilding Saint Peters basilica. In Julius' time the basilica was old and slowly falling apart. Once when Alexander VI was holding mass a piece of the ceiling came down, which many people saw as an omen. The old basilica was commissioned by Emperor Constantine at the beginning of the 4th century. Julius decided to rebuild it. He got one of the most famous architects of his time to Rome to work for him. His name was Donato Bramante.

11.4 The ceiling

After this the pope diverted all his time and marble to the project of the new church and the pope lost interest in Michelangelo's work on his tomb. Instead he thought it would be a good idea to get Michelangelo to paint the ceiling of his uncle's chapel, the Sistine chapel. Michelangelo was very reluctant to take this commission, because he did not consider himself a painter. He thought of himself mainly as a sculptor. In fact, he was so angry that when the pope was not paying attention he left for Florence and the pope had to send people to get him back. He made Michelangelo sign the contract, which he stubbornly signed: the sculptor Michelangelo.

But, even though Michelangelo did not consider himself a painter and had never really painted fresco before, he managed to create one of the most important fresco paintings ever made. Michelangelo had the capacity to become extremely good at something in a very short period of time.

Why did the pope have this strange idea to get his greatest sculptor to paint? Some say the idea came from the architect of the new Saint Peter, Bramante. He wanted to see Michelangelo fail, which would have been a logical outcome since fresco painting is a very difficult technique. Bramante hoped then to be able to convince the pope to give the commission to one of his protégées, the young unknown Raphael from Urbino. This plan of course failed completely because of Michelangelo's genius. Raphael still got to work in the Vatican though. Julius gave him the commission to paint his private quarters, the Raphael Rooms you have visited before coming to the Sistine Chapel (unless you took the shortcut).

11.5 The subject

The pope wanted a complex ceiling with many different layers of meaning. Michelangelo gave him precisely that. Michelangelo decided to paint nine scenes from the book of Genesis.

11.6 The four corners

In the four corners we can see four miraculous salvations of the Jewish people. You can see scenes from the stories of the brazen serpent, the punishment of Haman, David and Goliath and Judith and Holofernes.

11.7 The niches

Within the niches you can see people sitting and lying down. These people symbolize the people that lived before Christ. They look bored and trapped in time. They are symbolically waiting for Christ to come and release them from the original sin.

11.8 Prophets and Sibyls

Then you can see big figures of prophets from the Old Testament and female sibyls, who are pagan prophetesses. These figures prophesize the coming of Christ. Why did Michelangelo also paint pagan figures? In the renaissance people thought that even in roman and Greek times there were signs about the coming of Christ. The people just did not know how to interpret these signs.

11.9 Jonah

Jonah is also painted. He is a very big figure due to his importance and connection to Christ. Jonas stayed three days inside the whale, Lazarus was resurrected by Jesus after three days and Jesus was resurrected after three days. So all these figures point to the coming of Christ. Christ is never painted but everything in the fresco points to Him.

11.10 Ignudi

You can also see a lot of naked people. They are called *ignudi*, which is Italian for naked people. Do you remember the Torso Belvedere, the statue without head, arms and feet we saw before? All these naked figures are different interpretations of that statue. We can see Michelangelo imagining what the statue would have looked like.

11.11 The drunkenness of Noah

The first three scenes that Michelangelo painted are scenes from the life of Noah. You can see he painted these scenes first. Why? Look at them. Look at the figures. What can you see when you compare these figures with the figures he painted later? These figures are much smaller. He painted these scenes, took down the scaffolding and looked up. He saw that the figures are too small to make a big impression. So for the next six scenes he painted the figures much bigger. And of course he was right, because those scenes are the scenes we all remember and by postcards and posters of, like the creation of man.

The first scene depicts the drunkenness of Noah. This is a story that takes place after the flood. We see him first working in the vineyard, and then, after making wine he gets drunk and passes out completely naked. Ham, his son goes inside his tent and sees his father naked. He then goes out and tells his brothers about it, who go into Noah's tent and cover him up without looking at him. When Noah wakes up, he then curses Noah's son Canaan, who becomes the ancestor of the enemies of Israel, the Canaanites. This is a complicated story and even biblical scholars are not quite sure what it means. Why Michelangelo painted this here I will tell you later.

11.12 The Deluge

Then in the next scene we see the flood. It rained forty days and forty nights, because God wanted to rid the earth of the wicked people. Only Noah and his family were allowed to stay alive. We see the Ark Noah built and in the foreground the last humans who try to escape the flood by climbing the highest mountains.

11.13 The sacrifice of Noah

The next scene shows The Sacrifice of Noah. Noah built an altar and sacrificed a ram to God to thank Him for saving him from the flood. If you look closely you can see there is a part missing. The ceiling was damaged because of an explosion at Castel Sant'Angelo in 1797 when Napoleon invaded Rome.

11.14 Adam and Eve

The next cycle shows scenes from the life of Adam and Eve. As I said before, you can clearly notice the difference in style between the scenes of Noah and the rest. These figures are a lot bigger and are far more impressive. The scenes are not as complicated. This makes the compositions are a lot more striking. The creation of Adam, which is probably the most famous scene in the entire fresco painted in one day.

11.15 Fresco painting

The technique of fresco painting is very difficult. You do not just paint on the wall, because then over time the paint will fall down. You have to paint on fresh plaster. The word *fresco* means fresh in Italian. Then when the plaster dries the paint is stuck inside. So you paint in the wall and not on the wall. This means every day the painter has to apply as much plaster as he is going to paint on that day. Michelangelo first would make life size sketches on paper and then put tiny holes in the lines of the drawing. He would then blow charcoal through the hole on the wet plaster. During the restoration it came to light that he stopped using this technique after a while and started painting directly on the ceiling. So you can see his technique improving. Very few painters were capable of painting directly on the plaster without making mistakes.

11.16 The creation of Man

In this fresco we see God creating man with the touch of a finger. He puts life in him through a touch. This is a very original composition. This was never before painted like this.

Look at the shape behind God. What does this remind you of? A few years ago a neurologist wrote a famous essay about this form. He was convinced this form is a pretty accurate cross-section of a human brain. This is very well possible, because Michelangelo was one of the very few people in Europe who had studied corpses. He had gotten special permission to dissect dead bodies. So he would have known what a brain looks like. So the idea here is that all creation was already in God's brain when he created Adam. And you can see eve and other people behind god in his brain, waiting to be created.

11.17 The creation of Eve

The next scene is the Creation of Eve. God decided that Adam needed a companion and therefore took a rib from him and created Eve out of this. We can see Eve thanking God for being created.

11.18 The expulsion from paradise

Then we see the story of the expulsion from paradise depicted. These is also a very famous scene. We see two scenes divided by the tree of good and evil. On the left Adam and Eve are tempted by the snake to eat the forbidden fruit, which in this case is not an apple but a fig. Also the snake is a female figure. Both Adam and Eve choose to eat the fruit. You can see Adam picking his own fruit and Eve accepting the fruit from the snake.

On the right side we see them both being cast away from paradise by an Angel. Can you see how Adam and Eve change? On the left they are young and beautiful but on the right they have aged, they try to cover their naked bodies, because they have learned shame. Look at their expressions. Now they have to suffer.

Now let's look at this fresco and compare this one to the ones made by the artists from a generation before Michelangelo. Look at the figures on the frescoes on the side walls and then to the figures in the fresco about the expulsion of paradise. Can you see a difference?

A big difference of course is that Michelangelo's figures are naked, but this is not the difference I am looking for. Look at the composition of the figures. Can you see the figures on the side-walls look like they are made from cardboard? They are very two dimensional. It looks like if you would blow, they would fall over. Now look back to Michelangelo's fresco. Can you see how three dimensional the figures are? Michelangelo's figures always have a lot of tension in them, which makes them look more alive. They are always positioned in a difficult position.

Now what do you think of Michelangelo's landscapes? Can you see any? Compared to the painters on the side-walls his landscapes are really bad. Look at how beautiful the landscapes of Perugino and Botticelli are. Michelangelo was a sculptor and what he did is just paint the sculptures he had in his head. If you look at all the figures on the ceiling you can see that they all look like three dimensional sculptures. This is why we are still talking about Michelangelo. He really gave life to the figures in his paintings (and sculptures as well for that matter). His art was also of a very important influence on the style that came after him, the baroque.

11.19 *The creation of the world*

The next three scenes show God creating the world.

First we see Him dividing the waters from the land and below that he is creating the sun and the moon. Here we see God turned around and creates the plants.

In the last scene we see him dividing light and darkness thus creating night and day.

11.20 The rest of the ceiling

Let me also point out these bronze people, they are waiting to be born. Michelangelo used the same cartoon; he just turned it over to save time.

The gold medallions were supposed to tell other stories from the Old Testament, but these were left unfinished because the gold was not available and the Pope could not wait any longer to celebrate mass.

11.21 What does it all mean?

Now what is the general meaning of all these paintings? The general theme is the coming of Christ. Like I said before, everything points to Christ even if he is not depicted himself. But there are more meanings. Why did Michelangelo paint these exact nine scenes from the Old Testament? This has to do with sin. The main door of the chapel is not the small door you came in through. It is of course the big, closed door on the other side of the altar. If you would come in through this door and you would look up what would you see? You first see the drunkenness of Noah. So you will see sin. Then the next scenes also have something to do with sin. God punishes humankind through a flood. Humans are expelled from paradise because they have sinned. But then as you walk forward and get closer to the altar who do you get closer to? Of course this is God, the main fresco above the altar is the beginning, which is God creating light and dark. So as you walk forward you get closer to god. Of course the altar also symbolizes God. So it is the human journey to go from sin to god.

11.22 The method

Michelangelo started painting May 12, 1508 and mass was celebrated on October 31st 1512. It took four years to paint the whole ceiling. Michelangelo worked 18 hours a day and ate and slept very little. He slept on the scaffolding he built and when he woke up he would continue working. After he finished he said he had difficulty straightening his neck and if he wanted to read a letter he had to hold it above his head. We have little sketches of Michelangelo where he draws himself painting. He was not lying on his back as many people believe but standing up straight, looking up and paint. Michelangelo describes his work in a letter to Giovanni da Pistoia: "When the Author Was Painting the Vault of the Sistine Chapel" —1509

> I've already grown a goiter from this torture,
>
> hunched up here like a cat in Lombardy
>
> (or anywhere else where the stagnant water's poison).
>
> My stomach's squashed under my chin, my beard's
>
> pointing at heaven, my brain's crushed in a casket,
>
> my breast twists like a harpy's. My brush,
>
> above me all the time, dribbles paint
>
> so my face makes a fine floor for droppings!
>
> My haunches are grinding into my guts,
>
> my poor ass strains to work as a counterweight,
>
> every gesture I make is blind and aimless.
>
> My skin hangs loose below me, my spine's
>
> all knotted from folding over itself.
>
> I'm bent taut as a Syrian bow.
>
> Because I'm stuck like this, my thoughts
>
> are crazy, perfidious tripe:
>
> anyone shoots badly through a crooked blowpipe.
>
> My painting is dead.
>
> Defend it for me, Giovanni, protect my honor.
>
> I am not in the right place—I am not a painter.

12. THE VATICAN MUSEUMS 9: THE LAST JUDGMENT

12.1 The last judgment

After Michelangelo was finished he hoped never to paint again. He went on and created many more beautiful sculptures but after 24 years a new Pope decided he wanted Michelangelo to finish what he had started. It was Pope Paul III who became a very important patron of Michelangelo. Not only did he commission him to paint the last judgment in the Sistine chapel, he also convinced him that he would be a good architect. So he made him chief architect of Saint Peter's, made him design a new Capitoline Hill and gave him many more projects.

Michelangelo was now in his sixties, He started painting the Last Judgment, the enormous fresco you see painted at the altar wall in 1535 and finished 1542. It took him six years to finish. Two windows from the altar wall had to be closed and other frescos destroyed, including parts of Michelangelo's own work.

The tone of this work is very different from that of the ceiling. The ceiling is about the coming of the savior. This work is much darker. It depicts the last judgment.

12.2 Christ

High in the middle of the fresco we see Christ. Now, does he look like the traditional Christ you see in other paintings? Not at all. He is beardless and very muscular. He looks almost like a classical god, which is not so strange to think, because Michelangelo used two statues we have seen earlier as a model for Christ. For his head he used the statue of the Apollo belvedere which we saw in the octagonal courtyard, and for his body he used the Belvedere Torso. He is a powerful figure. With one hand he raises the dead from their graves and with the other one he judges. He decides who goes to heaven and who goes to hell.

12.3 The angels

If you look below Christ you these wingless angels with trumpets. They awaken the dead. They carry two books. One book contains the list of the blessed souls and one of the damned. Can you guess which one is which? Of course the small book contains the list of the blessed. Only very few people will go to heaven, most will go to hell.

12.4 Historical background

The fresco has a very dark subject. This has everything to do with the time it was painted in. 24 years had passed since Michelangelo painted the ceiling and the positive spirit of the renaissance had faded. In 1527 the troops of Emperor Charles V had sacked Rome and Michelangelo was there when it happened. It is said this was the worst sack of the city ever, including the ones by the barbarians after the fall of the West-Roman Empire. Priests were murdered, nuns were raped, artworks destroyed. The unfinished basilica of Saint Peters was used as a stable.

Also in 1517 another thing had happened. In Germany there was an Augustinian monk who absolutely did not like the way the Popes were behaving. Traveling monks were selling indulgences in

Germany to fund the building of Saint Peter's and the many wars the Popes were fighting. If you bought an indulgence you could secure your place in heaven according to the pope. This monk started a protest and in 1517 he put 95 theses on the church door in Wittenberg where he lived at the time. His name of course was Martin Luther and he started the Protestant revolution. The Catholic Church lost many believers in the northern parts of Europe.

So the message in the fresco is beware of what you do. You have to follow the right path, the catholic path or else you are going to go to hell. Next to Christ we can see Saint Peter. His face is a portrait of Pope Paul III.

We also can see on the left side a figure who is pulled up to heaven by an angel using a rosary. Of course Luther had said that rosaries are useless, so this is a clear attack on Luther by Michelangelo.

12.5 Saints

Around Christ we see many Saints. On the right side with the keys to heaven in his hand we can see Saint Peter. This is a portrait of Pope Paul III. On the right side below Christ we see Saint Bartholomew. He is holding his own skin in his handed because he was skinned alive. Now if you look at the skin it is not the same as Saint Bartholomew. It is actually a portrait of Michelangelo. He shows himself empty and tired because of all the work he had to do.

Left of Bartholomew we see Saint Lawrence. He is holding a grill in his hand because he was grilled alive. He was martyred during the reign of Emperor Valerian. According to legend they grilled him alive and at a certain point Lawrence lifted himself up and said: 'You can turn me over now, this side is done'.

Above him you can see Saint Andrew with his back turned to us. He is recognizable by the cross he is holding which is shaped like an X.

Left of Andrew we see Saint John and to his right side you see Mary next to Christ. She turns her head, because she is sorry for the people that go to hell.

All these figures represent the most important Churches in Rome. Saint Peters, Santa Maria Maggiore, Saint John in Lateran etc.

12.6 More Saints

Above Christ you can see angels holding up his crown of thorns, the Cross and the pillar against which Christ was whipped.

Then on your right side you can see another group of saints. You can see Saint Sebastian all the way on the right, holding the arrows he was pierced with in his hand. Next to him is Saint Catherine of Alexandria, holding the wheel which she was tortured on.

Now if you would go to the Capodimonte museum in Naples you could see a copy of this fresco done by an artist a few years after Michelangelo had finished. The amazing thing is that on this copy all these figures are naked. These were all dressed after Michelangelo had died and in the rest of the fresco many private parts were covered up, because later Popes thought the painting was indecent.

12.7 Hell

Then lastly on the right side just above the door we see hell. People are brought to Hell on a boat by Charon, a classical depiction of hell. In hell itself we see a man with ears like an ass and a snake around him. The snake bites him in a very unpleasant spot. This is a portrait of Biago de Cesena, who was the pope's master of ceremonies.

When he saw the fresco when Michelangelo was working on it he said it belonged in a brothel and not in a church. This, because there were so many naked pictures in the painting. Michelangelo heard this and painted him in Hell as Minos, the judge of the underworld. Biago was furious and went to see the Pope to complain. But Paul III said that as pope he just had power over heaven, but whatever happened in hell he could not influence. So Biago is still there.

12.8 Restoration

The chapel was restored between 1981 and 1993. It took 12 years to restore what one man painted in ten years. The company that paid for the restoration was Nippon, a Japanese TV network. They paid 100 million dollars. It took hundred experts to restore everything. What Nippon asked for in return was exclusive photography right of the Sistine chapel for 10 years. What the art historians amazed the most after the restoration was done were the colors of the chapel. It turned out Michelangelo had used much brighter colors than anybody had ever believed. Because of candle smoke the frescoes had become dark, but when they were restored people at first thought the restorers had repainted the ceiling.

12.9 The Sistine Chapel today

The Sistine Chapel is still used today for ceremonies like the election of the Pope. This is called a conclave, which comes from the Latin Cum Clave, which means with key. The cardinals are locked inside the chapel. In earlier times this was to make them quickly choose a new Pope. In medieval times it would sometimes take years before a new pope was elected, so at some point the cardinals were locked inside the chapel to make sure they would hurry up. During a conclave a little stove is put in the chapel and a chimney leads the smoke out through the window. The cardinals write the name of their papal choice on a piece of paper and then votes are counted by three cardinals. Then the voting papers are burned. Before damp straw was added if no pope was elected to turn the smoke black, but now they use chemicals. White smoke will appear from the chimney if the election is successful and nowadays also the bells will ring to make it absolutely clear.

There is a persistent legend the new pope must be checked if he is male by feeling his testicles. This is an utter fabrication, which comes from the legend of Popess Joan, which is also a legend and nothing more.

If a cardinal is elected he must first accept. After this he will go to a small room next to the Sistine chapel, which is called the crying room. Here he dresses himself in papal gowns. Three sizes are ready ever since John XXIII did not fit in his gowns. The new pope is then taken to the balcony of Saint Peter's and is introduced by the Latin phrase: Annuntio vobis gaudium magnum: Habemus Papam, which means I announce to you a great joy, we have a Pope.

12.10 Exit

There are two exits in the Sistine Chapel. Make sure you know which one you want to take, because once you are out, you are not allowed to get back in. The door on the far right in the corner leads you to Saint Peter's Basilica. This door is normally reserved for tour groups with a guide, but most of the time you can use it without problems. If you take this door, you cannot get back into the museums. Did you leave your backpack at the luggage room at the entrance? If so, you have to walk back from Saint Peter's Square outside the Vatican to the entrance of the Museums. The good thing about this door is that you will not have to do the line to enter Saint Peter's Basilica. These days, the line to enter the Basilica are very long, because people have to go through security again. So this shortcut can save you a lot of time.

If you already saw Saint Peter's or you want to go back to the beginning of the museum, you can take the door in the middle on the left (always with you back to the Last Judgement and the Altar). This door leads you through some nice halls back to the hall with the long escalator where you came in. You can find the restaurants here, the Vatican Post and the souvenir shops. After, you take the beautiful double staircase down to the exit.

Just make sure to know where you want to go before you choose a door, because once you pass one, you cannot get back.

Printed in Great Britain
by Amazon